Signs of Cherokee Culture

Signs of Cherokee Culture

Sequoyah's Syllabary
in Eastern Cherokee Life

Margaret Bender

The University of North Carolina Press   *Chapel Hill & London*

Set in Cycles and Arepo Types
by Tseng Information Systems, Inc.
Manufactured in the United States of America

Some material in Chapters 2 and 3 and the
Conclusion is adapted from Margaret Bender,
"From 'Easy Phonetics' to the Syllabary:
An Orthographic Division of Labor in Cherokee
Language Education," *Anthropology and Education
Quarterly* 33, no. 1 (2002), © 2002 American
Anthropological Association. A summarized
version of some material in Chapter 3 is included
in Margaret Bender, "The Gendering of *Langue* and
Parole: Literacy in Cherokee," in *Southern Indians and
Anthropologists: Culture, Politics, and Identity,* edited by
Lisa J. Lefler and Frederic W. Gleach (Athens:
University of Georgia Press, 2002).

The paper in this book meets the guidelines
for permanence and durability of the Committee
on Production Guidelines for Book Longevity
of the Council on Library Resources.

Library of Congress Cataloging-in-Publication Data
Bender, Margaret Clelland.
Signs of Cherokee culture: Sequoyah's syllabary in
eastern Cherokee life / Margaret Bender.
p. cm.
Includes bibliographical references and index.
ISBN 0-8078-2707-X (alk. paper)—
ISBN 0-8078-5376-3 (pbk.: alk. paper)
1. Cherokee language—Writing—Social aspects.
2. Cherokee Indians—North Carolina—Social life
and customs.   3. Sequoyah, 1770?-1843—Influence.
I. Title.
E99.C5 B44   2002
497'.55—dc21   2001059821

cloth   06   05   04   03   02   5   4   3   2   1
paper   06   05   04   03   02   5   4   3   2   1

For Bobby Blossom

Contents

Illustrations

Preface

In 1992, I commenced research for a study of the Cherokee syllabary, the writing system for the Cherokee language completed by the monolingual Cherokee Sequoyah in the 1820s. I had a long-standing personal interest in the Cherokees, and I was interested in literacy in part because of my earlier experiences as an assistant second grade teacher and as a teacher of adult literacy. I was thus aware, before I ever went to the field, and even before I began exploring the literacy and orality literature in anthropology, that literacy was a powerful cultural resource, unevenly distributed in the United States, with extremely different cultural implications and associations for various groups in this society. I mention these experiences not only because they shaped my initial interests but also because they have lent insight to my fieldwork in ways that would have been hard to predict in advance. For example, the metaphor of the "code" that I use in Chapters 2 and 3 to describe a related set of modes of syllabary usage springs from my experience with codes used to teach literacy skills to young children. My experiences with adult literacy students made me sensitive to the possibility of alienation from particular types of reading and writing, or from whole writing systems themselves, and focused my attention on choices made among potential orthographies (writing systems) in classrooms and in cultural preservation efforts.

As a student of Cherokee culture, I wondered whether the Cherokee syllabary, a source of native pride with a unique history, might have a different pattern of distribution and different symbolic associations than does the roman alphabet used in the reading and writing of English. Influenced by the movement in literacy studies toward more culturally specific, context-oriented approaches, and away from a general linkage of literacy as a singular technology with particular types of cognition (e.g., "logical thought") and social organization (e.g., "civilization"), I set out to look for a "Cherokee ideology of literacy."

In the course of my investigation, I have learned the following: (1) There is no one Cherokee ideology of literacy but rather a range of specific ideologies that become apparent in different types and contexts of usage. (2) "Literacy" as associated with the Cherokee language is a multifaceted phenomenon, pertaining not only to the syllabary as a system but to a variety of styles of phonetic writing and in which reading, handwriting, and printing all have different connotations. (3) The various ideologies connected with literacy in Cherokee are not sociopolitical ideologies external to writing and, more generally, to language itself, that somehow penetrate or permeate language use; rather, language use itself is ideological, enacting categories that structure the Cherokee social world.

Before I began this project, I hoped it would branch out from the potentially narrow approach of literacy studies to address the current nature of Cherokee cultural identity more broadly, but I could not then have envisioned exactly the form that the relationship—between writing in the syllabary and Cherokee culture more broadly—would take. At that time, I hoped to work ultimately with an Oklahoma community, perhaps doing some comparative study in North Carolina or spending some time doing language study in North Carolina before a more intensive field study in Oklahoma. The rationale for this plan was that I would find more fluent speakers in Oklahoma and hence more—and a greater variety of—syllabary usage in Oklahoma. The North Carolina community, I felt, was so heavily characterized by tourism and so predominantly English-speaking that use of the syllabary might be absent or limited.

But I went to North Carolina first and decided to stay. The Cherokee language is still spoken by more Eastern Cherokees than most outsiders realize. In fact, I found that tourism itself played a major part in the fascinating cultural dynamics surrounding local language use and literacy.

Among the most prominent themes that have emerged in my work are secrecy, privacy, and protection. Although I am not suggesting that tourism created these dynamics in Eastern Cherokee culture, it is certainly an integral part of their playing out. For it is by way of the movement among, and differences between, the various contexts of syllabary usage that the potential for privacy, secrecy, and protection is created in a community of a few thousand visited by millions of outsiders each year.

Cherokee, North Carolina, is a community of many faces, only some of which are visible to the tourist passing through. So the syllabary appears in somewhat different modes of usage and presentation in the tourist shops in downtown Cherokee than it does in Cherokee language education, in local churches, and in homes. It is in the movement among these contexts that a range of Cherokee cultural identities (some relatively more public and some relatively more private) is negotiated.

This is all to say that some of the very factors that made me reluctant to work in North Carolina — the tourism, and the seeming inaccessibility of dimensions of the community beyond tourism — ultimately became integral aspects of my topic.

*   *   *

THERE SEEMS TO BE a generational cycle to the study of the Eastern Cherokees. James Mooney and Frans Olbrechts worked in this community in the latter part of the nineteenth and early twentieth centuries, collecting myths and sacred formulas and studying local knowledge of traditional spirituality and medicine (Mooney 1982; Mooney and Olbrechts 1932). William Gilbert (1943) carried out a genealogical study of the community in the 1930s that focused on kinship, and the University of North Carolina's cross-cultural laboratory, headed by John Gulick (1960), produced (or served as a departure point for) several studies in the 1950s and early 1960s, including the work of Ray Fogelson, Charles Holzinger, Harriet Kupferer, Paul Kutsche, and Bob Thomas. (See Gulick 1960 for a bibliography of papers generated by the project.) In the 1970s, Sharlotte Neely (1991) conducted research with the Snowbird community, an outlying Eastern Cherokee community that is considered to be highly traditional. The 1990s produced a new crop of ethnographic projects. Sarah Hill, in American studies, conducted work on Cherokee basketry that combined ethnographic and historical perspectives on Cherokee women (1997). Doris Hipps, in education, conducted research on contemporary attitudes toward formal education (1994). Lisa Lefler, an anthropologist, included a study of contemporary healing and cultural revitalization among the Eastern Band in her dissertation (1996).

I hope that my work has filled a niche in this body of literature. Although this book has literacy as its theme and focus, writing it has required the exploration of nearly all aspects and contexts of contemporary Cherokee life—education, tourism, and religious and social gatherings—and it has required me to visit an extremely diverse set of members from every Cherokee subcommunity. I believe, therefore, that it presents a more comprehensive and integrative view of contemporary Cherokee life and culture than one might at first suppose. In addition, although two grammars and a dictionary based on Eastern Cherokee data were produced as dissertations in the 1970s, few studies have focused extensively on the nature of Eastern Cherokee language use as it relates to Cherokee culture more broadly. Finally, because my work deals extensively with the multiple associations of the syllabary with different religious practices, I feel that it sheds light on the changing nature of locally defined concepts of religious tradition. In particular, interesting contrasts emerge with the earlier work of Fogelson (1980) in terms of the syllabary's role as an index of spiritual practice and traditionalism.

I am also hopeful that my book will be useful not only to anthropologists interested in the study of literacy and to Cherokee scholars but also to designers and implementers of Native American language education programs. I suggest that, at least in the Cherokee case, the associations of a native-developed syllabary and those of various other writing systems used in language classrooms are not the same and indeed may stand in tension with each other. This may be of interest to language teachers as they consider whether and how to include reading and writing in their classes and as they choose among the available writing systems.

*   *   *

I LIVED NEAR the Cherokee community in western North Carolina from September 1992 through March 1995. During that time, my fieldwork took a variety of forms, some formal and some less so. Upon first arrival in Cherokee, I worked at a local amusement park. This employment provided me with a quick introduction to the socioeconomic realities of the area and to the complexities of local racial, ethnic, and class relations.

From November 1992 through March 1995, I taught one or more social science courses at the local community college and the local university. Teaching brought me into contact with some members of the Cherokee community and also gave me a comprehensible "hat" to wear.

From September 1993 through August 1995, I assisted with a local Cherokee language preservation and education project. Working on this project enabled me to see the syllabary in use firsthand, improved my understanding of the Cherokee language, strengthened my ties to the community, and allowed me to make some modest contributions to the community from which I learned so much. I was responsible for building up a hypertext Cherokee language dictionary, a database in which entries included text, graphics, and sound files. This experience heightened my awareness of the need for anthropologists and linguists to coordinate their efforts with those of native language educators and to search for the areas in which their goals overlap.

From the time I arrived, I took for credit or sat in on whatever adult Cherokee language courses were available. These classes provided the basis for my learning of the Cherokee language, and I am indebted to their teachers. But they also enabled me to see what role the syllabary is held to play in language use and language learning by a variety of speakers and learners.

My fieldwork also consisted of formal interviews and participant observation. For most of the spring semester of 1994, I attended and took notes during several of the Cherokee language classes offered at the Cherokee elementary and middle schools, as well as at a local public elementary school whose students include both non-Cherokee and Cherokee children. I conducted twenty-one formal interviews with adult syllabary users, designed to elicit their beliefs about and attitudes toward syllabary usage.

When the opportunity arose, I attended services and Sunday school meetings of several of the local churches in which Cherokee is spoken and the syllabary is taught or used. I observed Cherokee tribal council meetings at which a Cherokee note-taker and interpreter was always present. In my attempts to determine the role played by the syllabary in Cherokee tourism, I conducted a door-to-door investigation of Cherokee's tourist shops, looking for syllabary-related products and talking with owners or staff when possible. Of course, I learned the most about Cherokee language and life from the community members who became friends over the years. I am deeply grateful to these friends for the knowledge and experiences they shared with me.

*   *   *

WHILE CONDUCTING MY RESEARCH, I attended a session on Native American women at the 1994 Annual Meeting of the Society for Ethnohistory (since published as Harkin and Kan 1996) at which Native Americanists were encouraged by several members of the audience to select and design their research projects in response to priorities set by local communities. Some of the anthropologists present pointed out that the questions addressed by anthropologists and the goals and needs of local communities may not always be the same. The anthropologists generally resisted the notion that projects shaped primarily by the discipline's needs and directions should be abandoned.

The dialogue at this meeting resonated strongly with me and reminded me that my own concerns about how to integrate service, relevance, and representation into my work are concerns that face the discipline as a whole. Meeting the needs of the communities in which we work while also meeting the demands of academic disciplines and careers can be difficult. I tried, however, to find a way to serve the community in which I worked while carrying out a project that probably would not have been designed from the inside. I learned quite a bit while working on the local language project; in particular, it informed the discussion in Chapter 4 of metalinguistic characterizations of the syllabary. At the same time, my interest in the syllabary and ability to contribute time to the project, a fairly unusual combination locally, allowed me to be of service. Thus my own interest in literacy was transformed in the course of my research into a resource for meeting the needs of the local community. But I am not sure that that could have been foreseen or planned.

Negotiations similar to those taking place at the 1994 ethnohistory meeting, having ultimately to do with who should represent whom in writing and in what fashion, seem likely to arise wherever writing is used for representation, as the syllabary is among the Eastern Cherokees. I think it is fairly clear that the study of such negotiations quickly leads to a consideration of central cultural issues such as power relations, the setting of boundaries, and the nature of shared group identity. These issues are not tangential to the study of Cherokee literacy; they are among the core issues addressed in this book.

*   *   *

MANY THANKS GO to Raymond D. Fogelson, Michael Silverstein, and Anne Terry Straus at the University of Chicago, who read multiple earlier versions of this book. Very helpful comments were also received along the way from Sarah Hill, Ray DeMallie, Fred Gleach, Morris Foster, Circe Sturm, Ross Hassig, and Deborah Cohen. Financial support for my initial research was gratefully received from the Spencer Foundation's Dissertation Fellowships Program, the Phillips Fund of the American Philosophical Society, and Fred Gleach, who gave me a loan when I really, really needed one. Greatest thanks go to the many Cherokee individuals who welcomed me into their homes and places of work and worship, to the Cherokee Language Project, and to the Cherokee Central Schools. Royalties from the sale of this book will go directly to the Cherokee Language Project of the Eastern Band of Cherokees.

Note on Orthography

The orthography used to write Cherokee in this book (quotations excepted) follows Cook 1979. Vowels are represented by the letters a, e, i, o, u, and v. The first five have the "Continental" values; they sound similar to the way they sound in Spanish. The v represents a nasalized schwa (like the French *un*). Consonants are written as t, k, kw, ts, tl, s, l, m, n, w, y, h, and ʔ. To speakers of English, the ⟨t⟩ sounds like the English consonant written as ⟨d⟩ and the ⟨k⟩ like an English ⟨g⟩, especially when they are between vowels. (Phonemes, sounds recognized by speakers as capable of creating meaningful distinctions, vary across languages and are captured differently by different orthographies, so there is not a perfect correspondence between the sounds represented in English and Cherokee with the same letters.) The ⟨ts⟩ sounds like English ⟨dz⟩ in most contexts and for most North Carolina speakers. The ⟨tl⟩ represents a phoneme that does not occur in English, but it can be approximated by pronouncing English /t/ followed by /l/. Most North Carolina speakers pronounce /s/ as [ʃ] in most contexts. ʃ is the International Phonetic Alphabet character for the sound usually written ⟨sh⟩ in English. The ⟨ʔ⟩ is a glottal stop, which occurs infrequently in Standard English, but may be heard in the word "uh-oh," between "uh" and "oh." Other consonants are more or less as in English.

Aspiration (the ejection of air following some speech sounds) is indicated by an h, and a colon (:) is used to indicate a long vowel.

Some syllabary characters in the text are handwritten to preserve necessary distinctions. The complete syllabary, with phonemic values, can be found in Figure 1. The reader will also encounter notation in the following forms:

⟨written form of a character, word, or phrase⟩
"written instance of a character, word, or phrase"

written instance of multiple characters, words or phrases, frequently from a blackboard or classroom handout

'English translation'
/phoneme or phonemic version of a word or phrase/
[phonetic (objective) rendering of a speech sound]
Cherokee word or phrase

Introduction

Why Study Cherokee Literacy?

This book is about much more than literacy. Literacy provides our entry point into a wider world of contemporary Cherokee linguistic and social practice. Because the Cherokee language has its own unique, indigenously developed syllabary, Cherokee literacy teaches us something important about Cherokee modes of communication and self-expression while enriching our cross-cultural understanding of what it means to read and write.

Three important arguments emerge as central to this book. First, although most Eastern Cherokees are not literate in the syllabary in the conventional sense, the syllabary plays an extremely meaningful role in contemporary Cherokee life through its broader semiotic functioning. Second, because the syllabary has been such a potent and polyvalent symbol since its invention, because it has been taken to represent both adoption and rejection of the dominant society's values and practices, and because it plays an important part in Eastern Cherokee self-representation through tourism and in other contexts, the syllabary is an excellent vehicle for the study of relationships between this community and the mainstream U.S. culture. Finally, the community's beliefs about the Cherokee syllabary, some articulated and some presupposed, shape usage of the syllabary in culturally specific and meaningful ways, demonstrating clearly that not all literacies are alike.

Syllabary Characters as Signs of Culture

In referring to the Cherokee syllabary's "broader semiotic functioning," I point to the ways in which the syllabary and its individual characters work as *signs*. The syllabary, invented by the monolingual Cherokee Sequoyah in the early nineteenth century, is one of four systems used to write Cherokee among the Eastern Band. As such, the signs that are its characters represent the sounds of spoken Cherokee. More specifically, since its characters are syllabic, each sign represents one commonly occurring syllable, a consonant plus vowel, in spoken Cherokee.

But if we stop here we miss several other levels on which the syllabary functions semiotically. The American pragmatist C. S. Peirce identified three kinds of signs—that is, three ways in which objects can be meaningful: as symbols, indexes, or icons. Syllabary characters, through their varied uses in Eastern Cherokee life, serve as all three kinds of signs.[1]

Following Peirce, a sign is *symbolic* if its meaning is conventional and must be learned. Most words are symbols of this kind, and so are the syllabary's characters when they are representing the sounds of Cherokee speech. For example, the syllabary character Ꮝ, which represents the syllable /ka/, works as a representation of that syllable only after the reader has deliberately set about learning its value. This value has been determined historically through the work of Sequoyah, the syllabary's inventor, and through the adoption and use of this character by literate Cherokees over the past two centuries.

A sign is *indexical* if its meaning depends on a more direct relationship between the object and what it represents such as contiguity, causation, or some other association. The music produced by wind chimes is an index of the blowing wind; my bundling up is an index of the cold weather. The reader will learn that the syllabary functions indexically in several ways: its use or presence characterizes users, contexts, texts, objects, and spaces, with a variety of specific meanings. For example, the syllabary is used in signs around the community to identify buildings as part of the Cherokee social and political infrastructure; these include a senior citizens' center, day care center, clinic, tribal council house, and so forth. The syllabary indexically marks these spaces as local, for Cherokees rather than for tourists. It accomplishes this function whether or not its *symbolic* meaning—the actual spoken Cherokee represented—is understood by those who see it.

Finally, a sign is *iconic* if its meaning depends on a resemblance to whatever it represents. Figure 1 is an icon of the syllabary chart published by missionary Samuel Worcester in 1828; a map of New York City is an icon of that city. The resemblance of the syllabary used in particular contexts to, for example, the print found in the New Testament contributes greatly to its meaning. The syllabary chart reproduced in Figure 1 is an extremely important local Cherokee icon, seen in homes, in schools, in books, and on products made for tourists, connecting contemporary usage of the syllabary with its celebrated invention and history.

Because of its rich polyvalence, the syllabary's distribution and use tell us not just about Cherokee language and literacy but about self-representation, social roles in the community, and local epistemologies. In Chapter 2, I will illustrate the indexical and iconic functions served by the syllabary in Cherokee language classrooms. The role the syllabary plays in communicating social roles and values helps to explain its importance in an educational environment in which other writing systems are in far more widespread use. Chapter 3 broadens this discussion to explore the syllabary's semiotic functioning in religious practice, cultural events, the local media, and the community at large. It becomes clear that the foregrounding of the syllabary's iconic and indexical functions, at the expense of its symbolic ones, serves to protect the community's most valued linguistic and cultural knowledge. I present community members' explicit beliefs about and attitudes toward the syllabary in Chapter 4, drawing on interviews with community members as well as participant observation in such contexts as a local language maintenance project. These expressed beliefs, such as the opinion that the syllabary is inherently more difficult than other writing systems, help to explain how the syllabary's symbolic capacities (as an orthography capable of representing the sounds of spoken Cherokee) have been overshadowed by its other semiotic qualities. Finally, in Chapter 5 I explore the syllabary's semiotic role in the complex context of tourism. Clearly, most tourists neither speak nor read Cherokee. Yet the syllabary is visible in signs marking the tourist-oriented downtown and on commodities produced for tourists. Under-

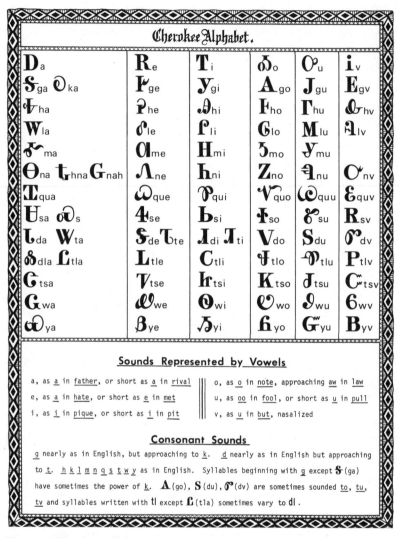

Figure 1. Cherokee syllabary chart, based on Samuel Worcester's chart, originally published in 1828. (From *Beginning Cherokee*, 2d ed., by Ruth Bradley Holmes and Betty Sharp Smith, p. 2. [Norman: University of Oklahoma Press, 1976, 1977])

standing why this is so and what the purposes and meanings of these uses of the writing system might be necessitates a grasp of the sylla- bary's capacity to carry meaning on a variety of levels.

Cherokees and the United States

Studying the syllabary also provides an opportunity to study the re- lationship between the Eastern Cherokee community and the domi- nant or mainstream society with which it is interconnected. Because of the syllabary's polyvalence, it should not be surprising that it simul- taneously provides a parallel to U.S. ideals of literacy, education, and "civilization" and points to a radical break with U.S. culture and its values.

No matter how "acculturated" the Eastern Cherokee population is considered to be, there is something to being "Cherokee" that is not co- terminous with being "American." Former principal chief Joyce Dugan was recently described as thinking "it was healthy—a miracle, really— that [the Cherokees'] native identity was still intact, still existed at all after the battering it had taken down through the years" (Gaillard and DeMeritt 1998: 26). This living cultural difference is strongly impli- cated in beliefs about how language use contributes to the production of various types of community members, how it marks community boundaries, and so on. The study of literacy in particular, because of its links with Cherokee history and self-representation, touches directly on the questions of how this cultural difference is maintained, how it changes, and how it might be threatened.

Language plays a crucial role in interactions between subordinated groups and the dominant society and more generally in power rela- tions among groups in society. In particular, writing has been at the same time a tool of the dominant culture's oppression and a tool of independence and resistance—and for many of the same reasons—for example, because it has been held by users to be an agent of "civili- zation." As discussed in detail in Chapter 1, the syllabary has always been a point both of connection and of disjuncture between Cherokee ideologies of literacy, civilization, and national identity and the corre- sponding ideologies of the larger U.S. society.

Other researchers have documented resistance to literacy in many

Native American communities, where literacy has often been seen as a threat to oral tradition. Willard Walker argued that "acceptance [of a writing system] by the target population is contingent on four factors: 1) acceptance of the innovators and others associated with the program, 2) recognition on the part of the native community that literacy is useful enough or fun enough to be worthwhile, 3) the acceptability of the content of any literature produced, and 4) the acceptability of the writing system" (1969: 149). Elsewhere (1984) Walker suggested that although the Algonquians of the far Northeast have traditionally used mnemonic aids in support of recitation, they resist the graphic representation of speech as a threat to their vital oral traditions.

William Leap (1991: 28–33) identified several reasons why writing is resisted as an element of Ute language preservation and education: (1) familiarity with Ute language literacy as a public phenomenon is not widespread; (2) the illiteracy of elders causes a generational role reversal among teachers and learners; (3) available reading material is limited; (4) literacy does not seem to have practical usefulness; (5) writing the Ute language is seen as an alteration of its condition as given by the Creator; (6) the spoken language is seen as unsuitable for representation by written text; (7) writing and reading to exchange information constitute a departure from traditional Ute information-sharing strategies; and (8) the uneven distribution of Ute language literacy likely to result from its introduction has the potential to complicate Ute social relations.

Because Cherokee literacy is an indigenous phenomenon, there has been a different cultural response. But the notion that literacy makes an indigenous culture vulnerable to intrusion and expropriation is still important in the Cherokee case.

Cherokee literacy occupies a central position in what is sometimes characterized as the triadic complex of hegemony, ideology, and resistance (e.g., Comaroff and Comaroff 1991; Philips 1998). Ideology is usually described as conscious and often politicized belief, whereas hegemony is "the invisible compulsion whereby context defines the limits of what is thinkable" (Hanks 1996: 205). In other words, hegemony exists when an ideology is accepted *as given*, without question or even thought, by people whose interests it may not serve. Cherokee beliefs about literacy emerge from a borderland at which a dominant culture meets a resistant one, a borderland characterized by a tension between conscious and unconscious beliefs, between acceptance of the dominant society's values and resistance to them. This means, among other things, that Cherokee beliefs about literacy and its connections to power and culture may be largely implicit.

The facts that something like 10 percent of Eastern Cherokees still speak Cherokee and that many still use the syllabary in specialized ways may in and of themselves be seen as evidence of resistance to the U.S. hegemony that asserts the centrality of the English language.[2] Most Americans presuppose the naturalness and inevitability of the English language—both of which have been to some degree rejected by Eastern Cherokees. Even today, there are elderly Cherokees who are more comfortable speaking in Cherokee than in English and many adults whose first language was Cherokee. But there is also an implicit acceptance of English underlying the community's orthographic preferences, as the reader will discover later on. And for some community members, U.S. English-language dominance is actually more explicit. One elder told me:

> If you go to work at Robbinsville [the town closest to a remote Eastern Cherokee community] plant, you got to speak English. If you gonna teach at Robbinsville, you gotta speak English, so . . . it's in other words, English—your way and ours, see. In order for us to live, we've got to live like you do, and we gotta talk like you do. We got to think like you do. And that's one reason why, you know, they're getting away from Indian culture, because Indians, here, reservation-wide, or here in Snowbird, they haven't got a thing. They haven't got a thing. Everything that they do is done in English. Every business that's carried out, done in English. Well, the tribal council, they got a Indian clerk up there, but most of the council members are, nonspeaking, you know, Cherokees. They don't speak Cherokee, most of 'em don't—just very few. So . . . in other words, there's no need for it. I mean, that's the way most people looks at it. There ain't no need of it. Of talking Indian anymore. Because, we live the white man's way, so . . . now you look around this room right here. You look next door, here, all you hear is just English language, you don't hear Cherokee.

But, the only place you hear Cherokee, in some of the older generation here, older people, but the young generation, they don't
understand it. They don't talk it. So . . . I believe that's the reason
why, you know, that the younger generation is shying away from
Cherokee culture and Cherokee language.

Although most Cherokees would probably agree with this older that
English is ubiquitous and indispensable, more and more are reject-
ing the notion that Cherokee language loss must inevitably accompany
the acquisition of English. In recent years, Cherokee language education programs and the language in general have gained a higher pro-
file in the Eastern Cherokee community. There has also been an increase in overt positive expressions of interest in Cherokee language
education by community members. Two new Cherokee language cur-
ricula were introduced into the tribally run preschool program and
elementary school in 1998, and a trial Cherokee language immersion
preschool class was implemented that year as well. A weekly Cherokee
language program also started up on local cable television. The syllabary has played an important role in this linguistic revitalization, with
more and more language-related commodities for sale in gift shops
and circulated among community members. In recent years, more institutional signs and billboards have appeared in the syllabary.

The syllabary's complex relationship to the dominant culture is no-
where more evident than in the public space inhabited by tourists,
where the syllabary serves different semiotic roles in marking spaces
and objects appropriate for outsiders and in marking spaces as part of
the genuine community infrastructure. The process of setting boundaries between community insiders and outsiders, between Cherokees
and tourists, is just that—a process, rather than a given. The Cherokee syllabary is of course not the only semiotic medium through which
these statuses are negotiated, but it is a fascinating one. It is important to understand that not all residents of the community or enrolled
members of the Eastern Band would necessarily agree on definitions
for such labels as "Cherokee" or "outsider," or on the specific individuals to whom they should be applied. It would certainly, therefore, be
inappropriate for me to suggest such definitions. But it would also be
beside the point because these are not categories with an ahistorical,

a priori existence nor can they always be understood as measurable qualities of specific individuals. Rather, these are the dimensions of contrast in terms of which the syllabary is mobilized to assert identity, to promote community, to communicate exclusion, and so on.

*   *   *

BECAUSE TOURISM IS SO IMPORTANT to the shape of contemporary Eastern Cherokee life and because the relationship between the tourist culture and the syllabary is both close and complex, it is important to think carefully about tourism as a site for cultural production and negotiation, as a vehicle for the—usually contested—representation of a community to itself and to outsiders and as a point of intercultural contact and communication. A generation ago, most of the interest in tourism in anthropology was of the applied, policy-suggesting kind, rather than of the descriptive, ethnographic variety warranted in this case. Cultural anthropologists may traditionally have shied away from sites of tourism because they felt they were somehow "inauthentic" and that studying such sites thus jeopardized the authenticity of the anthropologist. Anthropologists were supposed to study the traditions presumably inaccessible to tourists. They were supposed to get at the "real" culture hidden away from what Toby Volkman calls "the tourist gaze" (1990: 91). Perhaps because the Western appropriation of non-Western cultural artifacts and practices, as well as the exploitation of non-Western peoples, is considered by many anthropologists to be exemplified in tourism, and because anthropologists sought to distance themselves from such appropriation and exploitation, they sought to excise tourism from their fields of inquiry. In so doing, anthropologists perhaps hoped to dissociate themselves from the history of colonialism, social inequality, and dominance that has shaped modern tourism.

For many anthropologists as recently as 1990, tourism "seem[ed] to be a blight upon the local culture as well as an intrusion upon (and a threat to) the anthropologist's own privileged domain. As a phenomenon it [was] easily disdained, mocked, even condemned; as a subject of inquiry, it [was] easily trivialized" (Volkman 1990: 91). This trivialization was misplaced; dismissing the significance of an intercultural arena such as tourism was neither useful nor historically accurate. It was part of a broader historical tendency to treat as discrete the domains of the "native" and of the "outsider."

More recently, however, leading anthropologists have taken a different approach, teaching us "to reconfigure the usual binary opposition as a triadic historical field, including a complicated intercultural zone where the cultural differences are worked through in political and economic practice" (Sahlins 1993: 13). This kind of deconstruction of the rigid binarisms that have made tourism seem inappropriate as a subject of anthropological inquiry, along with a critique of anthropology's own relationship to tourism and the contexts in which it occurs, characterizes much exciting recent work (e.g., Adams 1995; Castañeda 1996; Davis 1999; Errington and Gewertz 1989; and Kahn 2000).

The popular and onetime anthropological assumption that tourism is *only* about exploitation and culture loss deserves special scrutiny. The anthropologist Marshall Sahlins's general critique (1993) of a trend in anthropology to read colonial situations as the wholesale imposition of the monolithic culture of the capitalist West on a consequentially dissipated or incoherent local "tradition" is pertinent to this more specific issue of anthropology's historical avoidance of tourism. The *cultural* interaction that occurs in the context of tourism is not a zero-sum game, which the economic interaction is perhaps more likely to be. The cultural encounter that is tourism entails a negotiation of boundaries, of identities, of particular material and nonmaterial resources. There may not be a clear or rigid demarcation between expropriators and losers of "culture." I am not at all denying that power asymmetry characterizes many postcolonial cross-cultural encounters. But such encounters may also be sites of meaningful productive activity for all of the individuals or groups involved.

It seems clear that tourism provides the opportunity for a range of practices that could only be described as fully "cultural." Tourism involves acts of selecting or creating, presenting, and exchanging artifacts and practices that the context designates as self-representational or as metonymic to the native self. The sellers also require a market, and they may cater to the fantasies and projections of that market. But the artifacts and practices produced for tourists can never be only a reflection of the desires and demands of the non-native consumers because the context in which they are produced differs from that in which the tourists formulate their desires and ready their gaze. Desires, or "needs," as sellers construe them, do not always emerge wholly from within the buyer's own culture either. Tourism may provide an opportunity for "natives" to indicate to "strangers" what their (the strangers') needs are.

In a study of tourism among the Toraja people of Indonesia, Volkman (1990) shows that tourism is not a discrete field of action but an integral part of the cultural life of a people, which undergoes change as a result of "old" cultural elements being set into a "new" arena. She demonstrates that certain practices and artifacts, notably a type of house construction and a type of funeral effigy, become differently valued and mobilized in the conjuncture represented by tourism in this Indonesian culture. These changes are internal to the culture, having ramifications in that culture far beyond the immediate context of tourism. Most important, in Volkman's work there is no "real" Toraja culture beyond the facade of tourism; what has happened to the elements of Toraja culture she discusses is treated as a productive cultural process, not reduced to "loss" or "corruption."

The creative and powerful ways in which the Cherokee syllabary is mobilized in the context of tourism exemplify this multifaceted cultural process. While it may be true that the syllabary's use in marking commodities and the landscape of local tourism exceeds its use in conventional "reading and writing," this does not reflect culture loss or degradation. Rather, it demonstrates the rich variety of contexts in which syllabic writing and printing are introduced and the plurality of levels on which this writing has meaning. In the context of tourism, the syllabary does the crucial semiotic work of representing, delineating, and protecting the Eastern Cherokee community.

A Unique Literacy

The final major argument of this book is that this community's beliefs about and uses of the syllabary have shaped its life as a writing system in highly specific ways, demonstrating that literacy is a diverse phenomenon.

This general point has been made before. Indeed, a whole minor industry in the human sciences has grown up around the question of whether it is possible to generalize cross-culturally about the impact of literacy on societies and on individuals.

Many of us who study the complex of technologies, artifacts, and practices called up by the term "literacy" are familiar with the idea, initially formulated by Brian Street (1984) but reasserted many times since (e.g., Besnier 1991; Newman 1996; Street 1993), that there are two central "camps" in the study of literacy. Each of these camps is believed to support a different model of literacy; in Street's terms, one of these models is "autonomous" and the other is "ideological."

Street identified as proponents of the "autonomous" model of literacy those thinkers who have argued that literacy itself, independent of historical context, brings about (or enables) changes in social organization at a societal level and in psychological state, behavior, or cognition at an individual level. Representatives of this model would include Walter Ong (e.g., 1982), Eric Havelock (1976), and most prominently Jack Goody (Goody 1968, 1977; Goody and Watt 1972). Elizabeth Eisenstein (1979) presents an extreme version of the "autonomous" model that emphasizes the power of print.

In a review essay on the topic, Carl Kaestle (1985: 16) summed up the characteristics of writing, which, in the "autonomous" view, are essential to its transformative power:

> Among the most important technological features of writing are these: it allows the replication, transportation, and preservation of messages, and it allows back-and-forth scanning, the study of sequence, deliberation about word choice, and the construction of lists, tables, recipes, and indexes. It fosters an objectified sense of time, and it separates the message from the author, thus "decontextualizing" language. It allows new forms of verbal analysis, like the syllogism, and numerical analysis, like the multiplication table. The long-range developments made possible by this technology have been profound, leading eventually to the replacement of myth by history and the replacement of magic by skepticism and science. Writing has allowed bureaucracy, accounting, and legal systems with universal rules. It has replaced face-to-face governance with depersonalized administration. On the other hand, it has allowed authorship to be re-

corded and recognized, thus contributing to the development of individualism in the world of ideas.

While authors like Goody focus on features such as those listed by Kaestle, framed as the positive characteristics of literacy, Walter Ong (1982) stresses the distinguishing and often positive qualities of *orality*. Indeed, he expresses regret at the depersonalization of communication that he believes writing brings about. Orally based thought and expression, he contends, have distinguishing and often positive associations. The oral is "additive rather than subordinative," "aggregative rather than analytic," "redundant or 'copious,'" "conservative or traditionalist," "close to the human lifeworld," "agonistically toned," "empathetic and participatory rather than objectively distanced," "homeostatic," and "situational rather than abstract" (Ong 1982: v–vi).

Street opposed these "autonomous" thinkers to enthusiasts of the "ideological" model of literacy, who deny both the straightforward causality and the uniformity of "literacy." Recent work of this type has also been called the "new literacy" studies (Brody 1996; Street 1993), and the figures associated with it include Scribner and Cole (1981), Heath (1983), Ochs and Duranti (1986), Besnier (1991), and Street himself. According to Street (1993: 1–2), the new scholars of literacy are distinguished by their acknowledgment of the multiplicity of literacies; the need to study broader social practices relating to and "local conceptions of reading and writing"; the diversity of ways in which members of newly literate cultures "transform literacy to suit their own cultural concerns and interests"; the relationship between literacy and modes of differential identity in nation-states such as ethnicity, gender, and religion; the importance of "vernacular" literacies; and the necessity of an ethnographic approach.

Street argues that the ideological model recognizes the centrality of "power relations" and "power structures" in its approach to literacy (1993: 7). Literacy, according to this model, operates at the ideological level, that is, "at the site of tension between authority and power on the one hand, and resistance and creativity on the other" (8).

It may be time to move beyond the binarism of this metamodel (this model of the models of literacy). The rich ethnographic literature on culturally specific literacies has substantially problematized the notion

that there is a single, universal trajectory from the oral to the literate (Bauman 1991; Halverson 1992). Furthermore, new theoretical and
methodological approaches may assist us in incorporating the study
of literacy into our broader anthropological projects of understanding the role of language in cultures, the relationship between types of
language use and forms of agency (e.g., see Desjarlais 1996), and the
articulation of language with other systems of meaning and value in
cultures.

We should treat literacy as a diverse human phenomenon with associated institutions, artifacts, practices, and ideologies, involving not
just technology and system but diverse forms of practice and distribution. Taken to its logical conclusion, this argument suggests that we
should not treat literacy as a neatly bounded entity of which exclusive,
targeted study is most productive. We must study literacy in the same
ways in which we study human social and cultural life generally.

Literacy practices, in all their diverse forms, are communicative
practices, in the senses articulated by William Hanks (1996) and
Penelope Eckert and Sally McConnell-Ginet (1992). Hanks has said of
this approach that "our starting point is the three-way division of language as a semiformal system, communicative activities as semistruc-
tured processes, and actors' evaluations of these two. . . . The three
elements come together in 'practice,' the moment of synthesis" (1996:
230). Earlier, Michael Silverstein similarly argued that "every linguistic category related to our ability to refer and predicate . . . is situated
at . . . a triple intersection of structural, pragmatic, and ideological
perspectives" (1995: 514). That is, as investigators of language in culture, we must keep in mind the three analytic levels—inextricable in
practice—of language structure, language use, and linguistic ideology.
Linguistic ideologies have been defined as "any sets of beliefs about
language articulated by the users as a rationalization or justification of
perceived language structure and use" (Silverstein 1979: 1). What does
this mean for the study of literacy? In studying literacy as a linguistic
and sociocultural phenomenon, we must attend to *all* of the following:
the structure of the writing system—its technical features and the specific ways in which it represents spoken speech; the ways in which the
particular writing system is used in a given sociocultural and historical context; and the beliefs about the writing system operating among

users. These three perspectives (ideological, structural, and pragmatic) are always mutually informing and interdependent, so that what may seem like the most straightforward aspect of a writing system—the way in which it represents spoken language—may be modified over time by both usage and belief.

In this book, I argue that the intersections and mutual influences of the syllabary system, local ideologies of literacy, and patterns of use must all be studied for us fully to grasp what the Cherokee syllabary means in contemporary Eastern Cherokee life. To get at the local meanings of literacy, it is necessary to focus on contextualized and concrete literacy practices, not only on the syllabary's nature as an abstract system. Observing usage of the syllabary in a variety of practical contexts—in churches, in classrooms, in the production of language education materials and commodities for tourism—has provided invaluable data. Moreover, I have sought not only to describe this observed practice but also to explore the dynamic cultural categorizations it reveals. Karl Marx said, "Language is practical consciousness" (Marx and Engels 1970: 51). If that is true, reading and writing are consciousness made tangible, circulable, commodifiable—and the importance of studying these practices and their products is as clear as the importance of studying human consciousness.

Local ideologies of literacy surface in interviews with syllabary users. Additional beliefs emerge more powerfully, however, from a study of literacy-related practices themselves. In the categorization and rationalization of their behaviors, members of cultures reveal assumptions about behavior that they would not necessarily articulate directly. By looking at syllabary usage, broadly defined, paying special attention to relationships among usage, context, and content, I have noted that the syllabary has local associations and meanings beyond those expressed in interviews. The set of associations that point toward the syllabary being a kind of "code," discussed in detail in Chapters 2 and 3, illustrates this.

The written word is a conveyer of specific meanings and general (symbolic) meanings, but it also has the capacity to be the source of or medium for practical transformations. In Cherokee, for example, writing has had the capacity to turn a medicinal formula into an inheritable commodity. Being able to write traditionally assisted in the transformation of a Cherokee into a practitioner of traditional medicine. Being able to read also plays a part in the transformation of a Cherokee speaker into a particular kind of Christian. This capacity of writing to serve as a vehicle for culturally specific transformations makes it an extremely rich field for inquiry.

And finally, it is extremely important to contextualize the study of Cherokee literacy in the unique history of the Cherokee syllabary. Doing so reveals why Cherokee language literacy is not just the meeting of a neutral technology—writing—with a specific spoken language. The life story of Sequoyah, including the ambivalent response of the Cherokee Nation to him, the almost immediate association of the syllabary with printing, the New Testament, and the newspaper that became a key site for debate over the removal issue—all these provide clues to understanding the meaning of Cherokee syllabary use, even in the present. This history is discussed in further detail in Chapter 1.

Some Background on Cherokee History and Language

At the time of first contact with Europeans, which was perhaps as early as the arrival of Hernando DeSoto (Mooney 1982: 23–29), the Cherokees probably occupied a large portion of what we now call southern Appalachia and its surrounding foothills, a territory that included parts of what are now Georgia, North Carolina, Tennessee, Alabama, South Carolina, Virginia, West Virginia, and Kentucky.[3] In the 1700s, it was reported that the Cherokees lived in several autonomous villages of a few hundred people each located throughout this region. Eighteenth-century Cherokee society was structured by membership in matrilineal clans and a pattern of matrilocal residence. An annual round of religious events such as the cleansing and renewing Green Corn ceremony was held in each village's ceremonial grounds, and medicine men cured illnesses through herbal and spiritual means. Towns classified themselves as "red" or "white" at any given point in time. A red town was in a state of war, under the leadership of young men. A white town was at peace, with old (white-haired) men at the helm. Women played an important role in the society, controlling the distribution of horticultural products, especially corn, and contributing to discussions in the political councils. At this time, however, the

Cherokee economy was already beginning to shift from one based on horticulture, hunting, and the use of wild plants to one more directly connected to the colonial (and then U.S.) market economy. Rather than hunting for subsistence, many Cherokee men were hunting for furs and skins to trade. By the nineteenth century, the U.S. government was pressuring the Cherokees to adopt white patterns of labor and social organization. Cherokees adopted plow agriculture, and new patterns of property distribution allowed major differences in wealth to emerge. In the early nineteenth century, the Cherokee Nation established a constitutional government, and many Cherokees converted to Christianity. It was in this complex context that the syllabary made its formal appearance in the 1820s.

By the 1830s, the climate in the U.S. Southeast had become inhospitable to the indigenous nations there, and a policy of removal was enacted. Southeastern Indians, including the Cherokees, were to cede their homelands in exchange for lands in Indian Territory, in what is now Oklahoma. In 1838, the Cherokees were forcibly removed from the original Cherokee Nation to the hilly northeastern section of the territory. It is estimated that one-third of the Cherokee population perished during this trip, which was undertaken in the winter months. As a result of the removal, most Cherokees now live in Oklahoma or elsewhere, but some eleven hundred managed to remain behind in the Smoky Mountains (Finger 1984: 29). It is largely their descendants who make up the currently enrolled members of the Eastern Band of Cherokee Indians.

The Cherokee Nation reestablished itself in Indian Territory and continued as a relatively autonomous entity until the establishment of the state of Oklahoma in 1907. In the late nineteenth century, land in Indian Territory was gradually opened up to white settlement, and Cherokee lands were allotted. This meant that land formerly held communally was parceled out to individuals and the remainder sold. Since that time, many Western Cherokees have lived in largely Cherokee communities, practiced their religion at Cherokee stompgrounds or churches, spoken the Cherokee language, and in general continued their cultural traditions. But there was and is no reservation in Oklahoma.

Back in the East, Cherokees also continued their traditional way of

life during the nineteenth century, and eventually the Eastern Cherokees obtained their own reserved lands in western North Carolina.
Most continued to engage in subsistence agriculture and hunting, and
by the turn of the century many Eastern Cherokees began to work in
the logging industry. By the 1930s, the area was developed for tourism, which has been a mainstay of the Eastern Cherokee economy
ever since.

Cherokee language use has been remarkably resilient throughout
the last two tumultuous centuries. Although some Cherokees have
been bilingual in Cherokee and English for a very long time, monolingual English-speaking Cherokees have been unusual until the last
few generations. In Oklahoma in the 1970s, the number of monolingual Cherokee speakers was sufficient to merit a bilingual education
program in the schools and translation services at public events and
institutions. In North Carolina in 1956, Cherokee was the preferred language spoken at home by all members of 41.33 percent of all households
in Big Cove, a conservative Eastern Cherokee community (Gulick 1960:
68–69). As recently as 1981 it was reported that in Snowbird, an even
more remote community, "the Cherokee language is spoken fluently
by most . . . residents over the age of 18. In a Cherokee-speaking family
the language is used at all times, even in the presence of non-Cherokee-
speaking whites. Cherokees seem to be very proud to know and speak
the language. Most children do not learn much English until they enter
grade school. All of the Snowbird Indians, except for a few older people,
are bilingual, speaking both the Cherokee and English languages. The
Cherokee language is very important to the Snowbird Indians, helping them to maintain their own tradition" (Wachacha and Wachacha
1981: 59).

Numerous government policies, particularly those enacted through
the institution of boarding schools that took children away from their
Cherokee-speaking families and in which students were punished for
speaking Cherokee, sought to eradicate the language over the course of
the twentieth century. Children kept speaking Cherokee even in these
harsh circumstances, however. Cherokee elder Robert Bushyhead re-
called: "About the time that we got that Cherokee language a'going real
good, someone would say 'I hear you!' They punished us in several
ways. They put soap in our mouths to wash out the language. Then

they even used a strap, or maybe had us walk up and down the side-walk in front of the entire school in a gown or a girl's dress, anything to humiliate us" (quoted in Friday 1998: 14–15CL). Another elder told me: "When I went to boarding school, and I was caught talking in Chero-kee, and they told me I had to wash my mouth out with Ivory soap, . . . which I did. And next time they catch me they told me they was gonna give me four-hour detail, that I would have to scrub the floor by hand, so . . . and after that, they tried to get me to forget, but I didn't. You don't forget your own language."

In addition to the boarding schools, the Cherokees' relative lack of isolation in both the East and West has also posed a threat to the Cherokee language. Still, this resilient language lives on through the strength and persistence of its speakers.

The Eastern Band in the 1990s

The core of Cherokee reserved lands is officially known as the Qualla Boundary.[4] Technically, the Boundary is unlike most reservations be-cause the lands were purchased privately on behalf of the Eastern Cherokees, although today they are held in trust by the federal govern-ment. Of the 56,573 acres owned jointly by the tribe, 45,554 make up the Qualla Boundary, 2,249 form the Snowbird Community in Graham County, 3,200 near the Birdtown Community are known as the 3200-Acre Tract, and the remaining 5,571 acres are made up by twenty-six scattered tracts in Cherokee County (Gulick 1960: 4–6).

A local source gave the total number of enrollees in the mid-1990s as 10,320, of whom 6,887 were reported to reside on Eastern Band land (Hipps 1994: 49). U.S. census data suggested a somewhat lower number of enrollees in residence. According to the 1990 census, of the 6,527 persons living on Eastern Band land, 1,094 were designated as white, 15 as black, 5,387 as American Indian, 1 as Eskimo, 13 as Asian or Pacific Islander, and 17 as Other. Sixty-six persons residing on tribal land were designated as being of Hispanic origin (U.S. Bureau of the Census 1990a: 88, Table 13).

Downtown Cherokee, the business and tourist center for the Bound-ary, is located in a valley at the foothills of the Great Smoky Moun-tains, where the Oconoluftee River is joined by Soco Creek, Wright's

Creek, and Shoal Creek. The Boundary shares much of its border with the Great Smoky Mountains National Park, and a section of the Blue Ridge Parkway runs directly through the Boundary lands.

The physical geography of the Boundary has been well described elsewhere (e.g., in Gulick 1960). The lands range from approximately seventeen hundred feet to five thousand feet above sea level and contain abundant timber, streams suitable for trout fishing, and some land suitable for subsistence agriculture.

The Eastern Band is served by a twelve-member representative body called the tribal council and a three-person executive committee consisting of a principal chief, vice-chief, and executive advisor. The chief and vice-chief are elected by the adult population, and the executive advisor is appointed by the chief. Two elected representatives are sent to the tribal council from each of six separate political communities: Yellowhill (downtown Cherokee), Birdtown, Big Cove, Wolftown, Painttown, and Snowbird/Cherokee County. In the past, these communities were served by individual day schools. They still retain some degree of social and political cohesion, as suggested by the existence of separate Head Start programs and community centers for each community. In at least some of these communities, community members still pitch in to assist families or elderly individuals in need with such chores as chopping firewood. This pooling of labor may go back to the traditional Cherokee economic cooperatives, known as *katu:ki* (Fogelson and Kutsche 1961).

The population of the reserve was fairly young in 1990, with a median age of 26.2 (U.S. Bureau of the Census 1990a: 513, Table 80). At the time of the 1990 census 66.3 percent of males fifteen years and over and 72.4 percent of females fifteen years and older were married or had been married previously (U.S. Bureau of the Census 1990a: 514, Table 81). Average household size was 3.1 persons (U.S. Bureau of the Census 1990a: 90, Table 15).

There are numerous Christian churches on the Boundary, representing a variety of denominations; Baptist church membership is the highest. There has also recently been a resurgence of local interest in traditional medicine and spirituality.

＊　＊　＊

THIS IS THE GENERAL HISTORICAL and social context in which the Cherokee language and the Cherokee syllabary are used today. It is in part *because* Cherokee speakers are in the minority today, with even fewer readers and writers of the syllabary, and because of the dominant society's ambivalent attitude toward Cherokee accomplishments, including literacy, that the syllabary has such semiotic power and polyvalence. The syllabary's complex history will be explored in further detail in Chapter 1.

Chapter One

Pride and Ambivalence

*The Syllabary's Received History
and Interpretation*

*T*he syllabary has never been uniformly seen as a straightforward, innocent, or neutral technology. At its inception, the syllabary was received in a variety of ways by a variety of parties —native speakers, missionaries, and Cherokee and white political leaders. Was it a blessing or a curse? Was it an agent of isolation or a tool for assimilation? Would it facilitate the conversion of the Cherokees to Christianity through the written word or interfere with the efforts of missionaries to teach English and provide a written Cherokee Bible? Would it assist the Cherokees in their quest for progress and development or prevent their access to the best that the civilized world had to offer? The tensions that surrounded its reception and use have not disappeared but continue to reemerge in the writings of historians, anthropologists, and linguists as they seek to categorize the syllabary and to describe its history. These tensions are furthermore evident in the current usage and packaging for tourism of the syllabary by Cherokees themselves, as will be discussed in later chapters. As a fellow anthropologist has pointed out (Terry Straus, pers. com., April 1995), the persistence of a tension or controversy may be a very important cultural persistence indeed. For it is within the parameters of such a conflict, in its terms, that much of what we call "identity" is negotiated.

The history of Cherokee reading and writing in the syllabary provided challenging exceptions to the dominant society's nineteenth-century rules about the place of writing in white-Indian relations. According to these rules, Native American languages were unwritten (until missionaries or other outsiders developed orthographies for them) and thus were not part of a "civilized" social order.

This dissociation of literateness and Indianness may have a long history. Michael Harbsmeier (1989) has suggested that in the movement of European society toward universal literacy, the production of images of a nonliterate other became necessary. The inhabitants of the Americas, represented in some of the earliest accounts as creating only noise and confusion, gradually came to be seen as having a specifically oral language and culture. This characterization of peoples as oral came to be meaningful only in the context of European self-characterizations as literate.

Peter Wogan (1994) faults historians for taking at face value early modern reports of Native American awe at European writing. Early accounts suggesting that native North Americans considered European writing to be inherently powerful and mystical contain projections, argues Wogan, of European ideologies of literacy onto a constructed oral other. This conception of Native Americans as categorically oral may in part explain the early historical treatment of Cherokee literacy as involving a brief, assimilative burst of energy with the qualities of a miracle and the focus on a few outstanding individuals.

The syllabary's history challenged this racialized, evolutionary scheme, but it reinforced other components of nineteenth-century literacy ideology. In particular, some aspects of the syllabary's history were used to support the inherent connection drawn between writing and "civilization." But while having its own writing system elevated the Cherokee language in many eyes, this fact did not seem to change the basic nineteenth-century American belief in a hierarchy of languages, cultures, and societies. To the extent that they were seen as literate, the Cherokees were no longer seen as Indian by the dominant society.

During the first Bush administration (1988–92), just before I began this project, literacy emerged as a focal point for charitable funding, volunteer action, and legislative efforts in the United States and was a major goal of international development efforts worldwide. But in the context of native North America, reading and writing had long been important symbols of power, progress, and culture. Indeed, writing may be seen as having played a central and formative role in the history of native North America. Treaties, maps, and the changing of official place names have all been means of asserting a new social and political order on the ground through written language.

The syllabary thus stands in a pivotal position—between the reinforcement of a hierarchy and its dismantling; between self-definition and external categorization; between independence and nationalism on the one hand and assimilation on the other. And as this book is intended to demonstrate, the study of writing cannot help but be the study of culture, history, and power.

A Brief History of the Syllabary

In the Cherokee syllabary, each symbol represents a vowel or consonant plus vowel, with the exception of the character ⟨oᎪ⟩, representing /s/.[1] See Figure 1 for the syllabary chart most commonly used today. Historians generally agree that Sequoyah developed this system in 1821.

According to many accounts (e.g., Foreman 1938; Mary Chiltoskey, pers. com., 1993), Sequoyah recapitulated at least one of the major steps in the "evolution of literacy." His early attempts at a logographic system were destroyed by a fire. It was then that he reportedly moved on to a phonetic (specifically, syllabic) system. But some accounts suggest that the recapitulation was even more thorough—that Sequoyah started with a pictographic or ideographic system (e.g., see Mooney 1982: 219).[2] Once Sequoyah perfected his system, he convinced Cherokee national authorities of its efficacy with the help of his young daughter. Father and daughter, separated so as to be out of earshot of each other, were able to exchange messages via the new writing system. This demonstration, followed by the successful training in the new system of several Cherokee youths, led to the general acceptance of the syllabary (Foreman 1938: 25).

Once the syllabary became public knowledge, literacy reportedly spread quickly, to the extent that a majority of the Cherokee people were literate in it within months. Cherokees began using the new writing in personal correspondence, to translate portions of the Bible, to

produce notebooks of medicinal texts, and for record-keeping and accounting. Political leaders, who had made use of translators to record
their proceedings and correspondence in English, were now able to
produce government documents in Cherokee. With the establishment
of a Cherokee printing press came the publication of the Cherokee New
Testament and a newspaper, the *Cherokee Phoenix.*

Despite the violent interruption created by the forced removal of
most Cherokees to Indian Territory in 1838, newspapers, religious materials, and political materials were printed throughout the nineteenth
century. In the twentieth century, however, less material was printed
in Cherokee, probably in large part because of the change in status of
the Cherokee Nation with the creation of the state of Oklahoma in
1907. Handwritten materials continued to be produced.

In the 1960s there was a resurgence of interest in Cherokee printing
(White 1962); at that time, some Oklahoma Cherokees participated in
the Carnegie Project, a native language literacy and education project
administered by the University of Chicago (Tax and Thomas 1968).
This project directly produced a variety of informational and educational texts in Cherokee; indirectly, it may have provided the impetus
for the use of the written language in a variety of symbolic contexts.[3]
In the mid-1970s, within a year of each other, a dictionary and beginning textbook were published in Oklahoma (Feeling 1975; Holmes and
Smith 1977). At the same time in North Carolina, a linguist and an anthropologist produced a grammar and a dictionary of Eastern Cherokee (Cook 1979; King 1975). Bilingual education programs were started
in both the East and the West. The technology associated with the syllabary continued to grow, and an IBM Selectric ball was developed for
the syllabary and, ultimately, computer fonts.

In sum, Cherokee literacy has been a dynamic phenomenon, associated with changing institutional associations, technologies, and contexts of usage.

Suspicion, Pride, Civilization, and Nationalism:
The Reactions of Sequoyah's Contemporaries

A story that appeared in the *Cherokee Advocate,* a newspaper printed in
the postremoval Cherokee Nation, gives us some sense of how Sequoyah's invention was originally received:

When Sequoya, the inventor of the Cherokee alphabet, was trying to introduce it among his people, about 1822, some of them
opposed it upon the ground that Indians had no business with
reading. They said that when the Indian and the white man were
created, the Indian, being the elder, was given a book, while the
white man received a bow and arrows. Each was instructed to
take good care of his gift and make the best use of it, but the
Indian was so neglectful of his book that the white man soon stole
it from him, leaving the bow in its place, so that books and reading now belong of right to the white man, while the Indian ought
to be satisfied to hunt for a living. (*Cherokee Advocate*, 26 October
1844, quoted in Mooney 1982: 351)

James Mooney, who collected myths among the Eastern Cherokees
during the 1880s, did not hear this story told himself, but, noting that
both Daniel Butrick and Elias Boudinot[4] recorded similar tales, says
he believes the story to be a popular one. Mooney reproduces the following, which Butrick obtained from an elderly Cherokee: "God gave
the red man a book and a paper and told him to write, but he merely
made marks on the paper, and as he could not read or write, the Lord
gave him a bow and arrows, and gave the book to the white man"
(Mooney 1982: 483). Mooney also quotes Boudinot as follows: "They
have it handed down from their ancestors, that the book which the
white people have was once theirs; that while they had it they pros-
pered exceedingly; but that the white people bought it of them and
learned many things from it, while the Indians lost credit, offended the
Great Spirit, and suffered exceedingly from the neighboring nations;
that the Great Spirit took pity on them and directed them to this country" (Mooney 1982: 483). This story of the book and the bow had fallen
out of circulation by the time Mooney arrived in western North Carolina. One might reasonably propose that the story was rendered obso-
lete by the invention of Sequoyah's syllabary. The poignancy of the
story is somehow lost once the Indians have regained what was truly
theirs to begin with. But it seems possible that a narrative could out-
live technological obsolescence if it continued to fit into or support a
specific cultural framework. If the narrative of the book and bow were
read today, a second reversal would be implied; the Indians, having
once lost what was theirs, have gained it back in spectacular fashion.

Perhaps the narrative of the book and the bow would have endured if it had reverberated with later Cherokee beliefs about the syllabary and about each people. But in fact, there are incongruities between the associations the syllabary has taken on in historical accounts, accounts by linguists, and accounts among the Cherokees themselves, and the associations it has in the versions of this narrative.

First, the narrative implies that reading and writing are, or were at one time, the natural gifts of the Indian. The prevailing beliefs about Sequoyah and the syllabary, however, posit the invention of the syllabary as a true miracle; many see it as a supernatural event of the highest order.[5]

Second, it implies a uniformity of "the book." The Indian had "it," then the white man stole, bought, or was given "it." From the very beginning, the new Sequoyan reading and writing was seen as very different from, and much more Cherokee than, the white man's reading and writing. (In Cherokee, the words for white man and the English language are related or, for some speakers, the same: *yu:ne:ka* or *yo:ne:ka*. To read English is thus to read "white.")

The first and third versions of the narrative also imply that reading and writing are fairly easy, that one must only have "the book" to be literate. In the early days of the syllabary's life, it does indeed seem to have been seen as miraculously easy to learn. Cherokee children who took up to four years to read and write English reportedly learned the syllabary in a few days and put it to use. But the reputation of the syllabary has changed considerably in the last 170 years so that it is now considered by many native speakers to be an extremely difficult writing system to learn and use. Depending on when this shift started taking place (and whether, in fact, all Cherokees ever saw the syllabary as easy), this may be another area of discord between the narrative and contemporary perceptions.

There is one area in which the narrative does reverberate with post-inception attitudes. The story was told to Sequoyah by his contemporaries, according to the *Cherokee Advocate,* to dissuade him from his project and to cast suspicion on it. Although the book was a gift from the Creator intended for the Indian, according to the narrative it has since entered the exclusive purview of the white man. The implication seems to be that there is something unnatural about Indians possessing the book. Yet that implication would seem to be in tension with the narrative's assertion that the book was the Creator's gift to the Indian in the first place. This tension between the perceived appropriateness and inappropriateness of Indian writing has colored the syllabary's history and can still be glimpsed today in local ideologies of literacy and in the treatment of the syllabary in the context of tourism.

The plural associations of the syllabary have always stood in tension with each other—both suspicion and pride have shadowed it. During the process of invention and afterward, the syllabary has been associated with traditional medicine and spirituality as well as with Christianity, and both have provided contents and contexts for its use. Sequoyah was reportedly accused of witchcraft while working on the syllabary, but once the system was developed, it was quickly put into use by *both* missionaries and traditional medical practitioners or conjurers.

Ultimately, then, the story of the book and the bow has been eclipsed by one much more complex. The narrative justification for why Indians do not write has been replaced by the story of the writing Indian. The original story of the book has been replaced by the story of Sequoyah.

It is fitting that this new, mysterious story of the book, the Sequoyah story, has been passed down in large part through the written, rather than the oral tradition. When I asked North Carolina Cherokees if they had heard any stories about Sequoyah, his life, or the invention of the syllabary, they usually said they had not. What they did know they told me they had gathered from the written accounts that began almost simultaneously with the emergence of the syllabary itself, which created an international sensation in the 1820s.

This story has become a legend itself, and it is shrouded in mystery. The firsthand accounts of Sequoyah are vague in both content and origin. Many of the early written descriptions of Sequoyah seem to be based on a supposedly firsthand account that appeared in the *Phoenix* by G.C., an unknown author. When John Howard Payne[6] tried to interview Sequoyah, his interpreter would not provide simultaneous translation, saying that he did not want to interrupt the flow of the great man's thoughts. The next day, Sequoyah said he did not want to repeat his story because his faulty memory might get him in trouble (Foreman 1938).

As Raymond Fogelson has pointed out:

> Important . . . in understanding Sequoyah's preeminence in the
> Cherokee pantheon of culture heroes are the uncertainties sur-
> rounding critical events in his life, lacunae that easily lend them-
> selves to mythmaking. Three such events stand out. First, there is
> the matter of Sequoyah's paternity. . . , The process of discovery in
> inventing the syllabary is also wrapped in mystery. The last days
> of Sequoyah are also subject to much speculation. In the summer
> of 1842, he set out with several companions to visit a detached
> band of Cherokee thought to be settled in Northern Mexico. The
> party got lost, and the old man was left behind while the others
> went for help. Sequoyah's mortal remains have never been recov-
> ered. Like Laotze and other great semi-mythic heroes, Sequoyah
> disappeared into the wilderness. The scarcity of reliable docu-
> mentary evidence, thus, makes the task of piecing together the
> facts of Sequoyah's life reminiscent of the quest for the historical
> Jesus. (1974: 107–8)

Fogelson's analogy is a powerful one, since most Eastern Cherokees
today see both Sequoyah and Jesus as important sources of "the word."

The etymology of Sequoyah's name is even a source of mystery. In-
terpretive translations range from "he guessed it" to "pig in a pen" (Kilpatrick 1965: 5); unlike many Cherokee names, this one does not enjoy
an obvious, universally agreed-upon meaning. Jack Kilpatrick has also
suggested that the name is a foreign borrowing (1965: 5).

Sequoyah's background has also been the subject of debate. Some
authors make much of his mixed parentage, insisting that his father
was the white trader and friend of George Washington, Nathaniel Gist
(Foreman 1938). Others have denied not only Sequoyah's white an-
cestry but also the notion that he invented the syllabary at all. Traveller Bird (1971) in particular has argued that the syllabary was invented by another tribe before contact and perpetuated by means of a
secret society to which Sequoyah belonged. The syllabary's very gene-
sis, then, is a source of conflicting interpretation.

Even according to the version of events that identifies Sequoyah as
the syllabary's inventor (all published accounts, essentially, except for
that found in Traveller Bird 1971), the Cherokee writing (now called

Sequoyan by some) emerged out of circumstances that seemed suspicious at the time. Sequoyah's motives and intentions were questioned; as mentioned above, many accused him of witchcraft.[7] His wife's relatives reportedly burned down the hut containing his earliest efforts, interpreting his obsession as, at the very least, an abandonment of his responsibilities. As one of my consultants[8] told the story, "He was half Cherokee, and not really full Cherokee. . . . I think by hearing people talk that's where he got the idea that we should have our own language, I guess. And then he worked so hard at it, you know, cause I think they said his wife burned his first batch of papers. (Laughing) And he had to do it again. So he had a hard time getting this together, in a way."

Grant Foreman claimed to have gotten the following account of Sequoyah's wife's and in-laws' reaction to his activities from the report of a doctor who served on the Trail of Tears, written after a conversation with Sequoyah's son: "[Sequoyah] constructed a hut in a retired location where he could carry on his studies in private. Constantly engaged in making queer marks on stones and bark and scraps of paper, and from morning to night making unaccountable and unintelligible articulations as he practiced all the sound forms of the Cherokee language, it is small wonder that his superstitious fellow countrymen became suspicious of him. Believing that he was engaged in some diabolical plan to destroy the nation they succeeded in drawing him from his hermitage, when they burned up his cabin, hieroglyphics and all" (1938: 47).

Missionaries to the Cherokees were also uncertain of the syllabary's value. They perceived it as a double-edged sword that could either civilize or further isolate the Cherokees. Adopting the syllabary as their major means of reading and writing might make Christians out of them and allow them to obtain all the benefits reaped by a literate society but would impede their contact with the rest of Western civilization and its written corpus. It would certainly, they feared, strengthen and prolong the Cherokees' attachment to their own language and culture.

Others were less vehemently opposed but simply did not understand what Sequoyah was doing. John Ross, the Cherokee political leader, referred to Sequoyah's effort as a "foolish undertaking" with which Sequoyah had become obsessed,[9] and Elias Boudinot, who was to become the first editor of the *Cherokee Phoenix*, was indifferent, ignoring the fact that the syllabary had become a functioning writing system in popular use (Perdue 1994). Both men, for their own reasons, would do about-faces on the value of the syllabary and about Sequoyah himself, but it would take some convincing. Perdue (1994: 122) notes that "highly acculturated Cherokees such as Boudinot had difficulty accepting a system of writing devised by an illiterate native speaker. They tended to favor the orthography of John Pickering, a noted philologist whom a Protestant missionary society had employed to develop a system for writing native languages and translating the Bible. The vast majority of Cherokees, however, would have nothing to do with Pickering's grammar."

Pickering's orthography was an alphabetic system that made use of roman characters.[10] It would have been convenient for English-speaking missionaries and other outsiders wishing to communicate with the Cherokee Nation, as well as for typesetters. But Samuel Worcester,[11] white missionary and lifelong advocate for the Cherokees, realized that the church and the agents of "civilization" would do well to go along with the people's choice: "Whether or not the perception of the Cherokees is correct, in regard to the superiority of their own alphabet for their own use, that impression they have, and it is not easy to be eradicated. It would be a vain attempt to persuade them to relinquish their own method of writing. If books are printed in Guess's character, they will be read; if in any other, they will lie useless" (Worcester quoted in Perdue 1994: 122). Worcester went on to praise the syllabary and to stress its ease of learning in comparison with English.

Boudinot would later not only praise Sequoyah for his invention but link it to the "elevation" of his people. In 1832, in an address to the American Annals of Education, Boudinot wrote, "It is not yet too late to do justice to this great benefactor of the Cherokees, who, by his inventive powers, has raised them to an elevation unattained by any other Indian nation, and made them a reading and intellectual people" (Perdue 1983: 49). For his part, Ross would go on to praise Sequoyah and present him with a medal "as a token of respect and admiration for his ingenuity in the invention of the Cherokee alphabetical characters" (Ross quoted in Foreman 1938: 8).

In the beginning, then, some reactions to the syllabary were ambivalent. Some Cherokees treated Sequoyah's project with suspicion, viewing writing as a supernatural gift rather than a neutral technology that could be invented and learned through inspiration and hard work. As the narratives above suggest, some felt that the Indian had lost the divine gift of the book long ago; how could it be regained now without supernatural foul play? But as Sequoyah's success in the invention became apparent, many Cherokees came to see the syllabary as "evidence of their spiritual worth, and their rapid mastery of it was an affirmation of themselves as a people" (Perdue 1994: 122).

There were doubtless other responses to Sequoyah's creation of which we know nothing today. Not only are we looking at the past through the selective lens of historical documents and the historian's eye, but, as Perdue pointed out (1977), there may have been a good deal of misrepresentation and selective reporting going on at the *Phoenix* and elsewhere because of the interest elite Cherokees had in presenting a "civilized" image of their people.

This image—of the Cherokees as foremost among the "civilized tribes" of the Southeast—has long been touted by scholars, in part because of the syllabary (e.g., Brown 1938; Foreman 1934; Starkey 1946; Woodward 1963). Among the characteristics usually listed to justify this label of "civilized," however, is a curious mixture of programs urged by the federal government or missionaries and taken up to varying extents and ends by portions of the population, actions on the part of a minority of Cherokees that may have been opposed by the majority, and practices that became part of everyday life for most Cherokees. It is also sometimes unclear whose view of civilization is being referred to, a "white" (e.g., U.S. government or missionary-inspired) view or a purported Cherokee view.

Two of the most widely referenced accounts of Sequoyah's life, Grant Foreman's (1938) and George E. Foster's (1885, cited extensively by Foreman), stress Sequoyah's role in uplifting his people from "savagery." Foster's book, fully titled *Se-Quo-Yah, the American Cadmus and Modern Moses,* is described on the title page thus: "A complete biography of the greatest of redmen, around whose wonderful life has been woven the manners, customs and beliefs of the early Cherokees, together with a recital of their wrongs and wonderful progress toward civilization" (Foster 1885). In this account, Sequoyah is seen as an inspired dreamer, whose invention is the "key of progress," both social and moral. Overall, the account is also intended as a testament to the miraculous effects of missionary work. Although this work was written while the Cherokee Nation was still an autonomous political entity in Indian Territory, it does not emphasize the *independence* brought about by technological innovations including the syllabary, but rather the *stature* given the fledgling Cherokee civilization by writing.

Grant Foreman's book, *Sequoyah* (1938), is less romantic and less moralistic than Foster's, but it still leaves no room for doubt that Sequoyah is to be remembered for bringing the Cherokees into the realm of American civilization.[12] "Most significant and lasting memorial to the immortal Sequoyah is the learning and culture of a fine body of Americans, the Cherokee people. Their advanced position in society directly traceable to Sequoyah's works, exercised a beneficent influence on other tribes of Indians and contributed substantially to the civilization of the new state of which they are a part" (Foreman 1938: 81). Foreman stresses that the Cherokees are Americans, contributing to the civilization of the new state of Oklahoma. Foreman's ideology of civilization is such that he feels a need to prove that Sequoyah's paternity is not only white, but of "the highest stock."[13] He writes, "Some writers [including Foster] have subscribed to the wholly improbable and unauthenticated theory that Sequoyah's father was a vagabond itinerant German named George Gist, whose rovings brought him in the Cherokee Nation. That the amazing genius of this remarkable Indian must have been sired by a man of vastly superior qualifications was obvious" (Foreman 1938: 75). Foreman goes on to attempt to prove that Sequoyah's father was Nathaniel Gist, a white trader and friend of George Washington. He even gives evidence of Gist's credentials as breeding stock, by pointing out that the trader's other children went on to make marriages at the highest level in society.

Foreman's and Foster's accounts remain classic, and the link between Sequoyah's writing system and the goals of civilized white society remains strong in many people's beliefs about and representations of Sequoyah and the syllabary. But later accounts (e.g., McLoughlin 1986; Perdue 1994) have departed from the view that writing brought Cherokees closer to being like civilized and, particularly, like Christian whites.

Many historians have linked the classification of Cherokees as civi-

lized with the following trends: the implementation of white farm-
ing and ranching methods, the development of private land and other
property ownership, nuclear family homesteading, the transfer of in-
heritance and familial authority from the mother's side to the father's
side of the family, and the outlawing of clan revenge (e.g., Foreman
1934; Woodward 1963). The Cherokees participated in such trends with
great variability, however (Finger 1984: 6–10). By 1821, a small group
did run large plantations and held a considerable number of black
slaves. But the vast majority of Cherokees still lived in communal
households, with women doing small-scale agricultural work and men
hunting, trading, and engaging in military activities when the opportunity arose (McLoughlin 1986; Perdue 1979).

The Cherokees' adoption of a constitutional government in 1820,
with judicial, executive, and legislative branches, is another example
often given of their civilized status. Because it is institutional, this
change may seem easier to identify with the Cherokees as a group than
the economic changes discussed above. But again, this institution did
not mean the same thing to all Cherokees, nor did they participate in
it equally. For some it reflected an emulation of, and attempt to blend
into, white society. For many it may have represented an attempt to
preserve a distinct national identity in white society. For still others, it
may have signaled a loss of power at the local village level (McLoughlin 1986).

The development of literacy in Cherokee has often been seen as the
pinnacle of this variously characterized Cherokee civilization. Like the
other developments discussed above, this one must be understood in
its own political and social context. Sequoyah was not an assimilationist; the sketchy data available about him suggest that he disliked
the changes whites and some Cherokees were trying to bring about in
Cherokee society and felt that his system could be used to make the
Cherokees more independent of whites.

It is important to tease out the different dimensions of opposition
and tension in attitudes toward the syllabary and toward the changes
of the nineteenth century generally. For a Cherokee to advocate something like progress meant perhaps some selection among and combination of the following: adopting white agricultural technology, advocat-
ing monogamy, developing a bicameral system of government similar

to that of the United States, outlawing clan revenge, and adopting some form of writing with which to record written laws and produce government documents. Adopting these practices did not necessarily go hand in hand with the adoption of Christianity or an abandonment of Cherokee traditionalism. Nor were such moves necessarily assimilationist. In fact, progress was seen by many as an aid to nationalism. People who opposed the syllabary did so for a variety of reasons, some of which were very traditional, such as the fear of its potential association with witchcraft. But there were those who opposed adoption of the syllabary out of their belief in the powers of civilization as well. Many more educated Cherokees favored a writing system, like Pickering's (Perdue 1994), that would more easily facilitate the transition to the reading and writing of English.

So it is not accurate to say that proponents of the syllabary were supporters of civilization or progress while those who opposed it were not. Nineteenth-century accounts of the preremoval Cherokees (and some later historical ones, such as Woodward 1963 and Foreman 1934, 1938) may make it seem that the syllabary was synonymous with "Indian improvement," but this was certainly not the only way in which it was received. Cherokee attitudes toward cultural change and Cherokee-white relations were complex in Sequoyah's time (as in our own) and varied by region and socioeconomic background. Technological, political, and religious change might each be viewed differently by the same person, change being seen as desirable in one area, inevitable in another, and unthinkable in the third. In considering each change, individuals might not just be for or against change but might be differently positioned along continuums like the ones suggested in Figure 2.

One's position along one of these continuums did not necessarily predict one's position along the others. One could certainly be a progress-oriented, separatist pagan—probably a good description of Sequoyah himself. Elias Boudinot could be described as a progress-oriented, nationalist Christian. Some members of the Cherokee citizens' reserves, Cherokees who traded citizenship in the Cherokee Nation for a reserve of 640 acres and U.S. citizenship, might have been described as traditional, assimilationist pagans.[14]

Could there be a Cherokee civilization that was separate from, equal to, and different from the fledgling United States? Elias Boudinot and

Area of Change	Pro-Change		Anti-Change
Technological	Progress-oriented -------------		Traditional
Political	Assimilationist ---	Nationalist ---	Separatist
Spiritual	Christian ---------------------		Pagan

Figure 2. Progressive-conservative continuums.

Samuel Worcester emphasized the potential for the Cherokee Nation to be separate and equal and downplayed the extent to which it was and would be different. The only element of the new civilization they sought to keep distinctly Cherokee was the language (although English remained the official and first language of the Nation). The articles they included in the *Phoenix* on Cherokee customs and history seem belittling. Yet politically, these men were fiercely nationalistic. There must have been other Cherokees, ones without printing presses at their disposal, who valued the writing system for their own reasons.

By defining themselves as literate, civilized, and indeed as an autonomous democratic nation, the Cherokees of the nineteenth century were engaging in some powerful political-linguistic negotiations about the nature of literacy, progress, and national cultural identity. Lee Soltow and Edward Stevens (1981) have shown that the context and ramifications of the spread of literacy in nineteenth-century America were extremely complex politically, sociologically, and moral-ideologically. According to these authors, nineteenth-century reformers in America implicitly accepted a hierarchical view of consciousness, in which literate practice became a form of consciousness raising, as "they sought to establish links between intelligence, virtue, and literateness in an ideology of literacy" (Soltow and Stevens 1981: 7–8). This ideology, spread through schools and newspapers, enabled reformers to link morality and intellect because literacy was not merely a tool, the acquisition of which reflected higher cognitive powers. It was also a medium, through which a certain system of values was expressed; the authors point out that reading is never just reading but always the reading of something (1981: 22). Thus as literacy was differentially distributed in American society, so too both intellect and access to a preferred system of values were held to be. Literacy therefore became a vehicle for social control, in the form both of social integration (the imposition of the values of one social group on another) and of social differentiation (the judgment and categorization of societal groups on the basis of literacy).

The Cherokee case raises the interesting possibility of a competing literacy, the use of which may presuppose or entail a system of values that is at least partially its own. Some elements of nineteenth-century Cherokee society were trying to establish themselves as literate and civilized in the heart of a nation in which, Soltow and Stevens suggest, the identification of literacy and civilization was a creative and ongoing process of social control. But while it makes sense to see these two processes (the development, distribution, and institutionalization of Cherokee literacy and the distribution and institutionalization of American English literacy) as related, it is clear that the shape of Cherokee literacy was not the result of a wholesale imposition of a mainstream system of values on a societal subgroup. Since other changes in social organization and behavior urged on the Cherokee Nation by various white groups (state and federal governments, missionaries) were adopted in highly variable ways and to various extents by the different sectors of Cherokee society, there is no reason to believe that the system of values associated with nineteenth-century American English literacy is fully implicated by Cherokee syllabary use.

Kathryn Woolard has shown that "authority and hegemony cannot be mechanically read out from institutional dominance" (1985: 743). The authority of a language, Woolard argues, "is established and inculcated not most importantly through schools and other formal institutions, but in primary relations, face-to-face encounters, and the invidious distinctions of informal, everyday life" (1985: 742). If this is true for language of use, it is also true for *type* of language use. That is, whatever linkage there was between Cherokee literacy and notions of civilization, progress, and enlightenment must have come to a considerable extent from the contexts of usage in Cherokee society itself. And this society was surely not exclusively a hegemonic reproduction of the larger U.S. society.

One would expect to find considerable resistance on the part of nineteenth-century U.S. politicians and educators to the possibility that the usage of Cherokee literacy could index a partially different system of values from American English literacy. If, as Soltow and Stevens suggest (1981), literacy in nineteenth-century America was a medium through which intellect was intrinsically linked with a specific morality, it would be very difficult to accept the linkage of what must be an analogous cognitive capability (via the acquisition of literacy) with a competing system of values. This may be why many accounts of the Cherokee writing system and of the place of literacy in nineteenth-century Cherokee history tend to deemphasize the counterhegemonic aspects of the syllabary and its uses.

Traces of these *other* associations with the syllabary, ones that have nothing to do with civilization as a nineteenth-century American value, may be seen in the attitudes toward and patterns of usage of the syllabary even today. The syllabary has a continuing association not only with Christianity, progress, and written law, but with medicine, animals and nature, and Cherokee place names. A Cherokee man told me that the syllabary was never supposed to change anything about Cherokee life or culture—it was "just a tool"—a very powerful tool, perhaps, but just a tool. From a culturally conservative point of view, then, the syllabary preserved culture and was not intended to change it. Part of the syllabary's popularity, Theda Perdue argues, lay in its indigenousness, a point also made by Mooney (1892). As a force of revitalization, it gave Cherokees a sense of pride and indeed was taken as "evidence of their spiritual worth" (Perdue 1994: 122). John Gulick notes that in the nineteenth century "the Cherokees' aim was to accommodate themselves to the ways of the whites only in such a manner as would peacefully preserve their independence" (1973: 12).

The tensions evident in nineteenth-century accounts of the syllabary are still evident in contemporary usage, as I will show in later chapters. In private discussions and in the underlying assumptions revealed in the classroom, both caution toward and pride in the syllabary are revealed. In many contexts, including formal language education, the syllabary seems to be almost avoided. Nevertheless, the community's pride in it is revealed in the homage paid to Sequoyah, the many portraits and syllabary charts that adorn homes, and the syllabary T-shirts that are produced every year for students.

In Cherokee, North Carolina, today, there is a tendency to stress both the importance of the syllabary and, if not its faults, its inherent inaccessibility. Yet in all aspects of language education, the syllabary is included, and no educational material or program seems to be considered complete without some presentation of the syllabary. This multi-layered treatment of the syllabary suggests the influence of both scholars of the Cherokee language who have emphasized the syllabary's limitations or omitted it from their work altogether (e.g., Pickering, in Krueger 1963) and those who have treated the syllabary as an integral part of their subject (e.g., Chafe and Kilpatrick 1963; Feeling and Pulte 1975; Holmes and Smith 1977; Scancarelli 1992, 1996a, 1996b; Walker 1975; Walker and Sarbaugh 1993; White 1962). Students (at the elementary and high schools, and in adult education) are expected to be familiar with the syllabary. This may mean only that they are visually exposed to it or that they are capable of looking up phonetic values on a syllabary chart. For some high school and adult students, it may mean that they are expected to memorize, for a time, the phonetic values of the characters. But rarely does it mean that the syllabary characters replace phonetic writing, and I never saw syllabic writing used to teach grammar or large amounts of vocabulary.

James Mooney argued erroneously, it turns out, that while Cherokees were unlikely to adopt any other writing system for their own language, the syllabary would not be in use much longer either:

When Sequoyah's alphabet was invented, seventy years ago, the Gulf States, the Ohio valley, and the Great West were all Indian country, and the Indian languages had a commercial and even a political importance. Now, all this is changed. There are today in the Cherokee Nation nearly two thousand white citizens, while those with one-half or more of white blood constitute by far the majority of the tribe. Many of the leading men of the nation are unable to speak the language, while the legislative and court proceedings, the national records, and the national education are all in English, and the full-blood, who cannot speak English, is fast becoming a rarity. The Cherokees are rapidly becoming white men, and when the last full-bloods discard their old alphabet — which they love because it is Indian — they will adopt that of the ruling majority. (1892: 64)

Mooney was suggesting that the Cherokee syllabary would be replaced not by another system for writing Cherokee but by the universal use of written English. Time has proven Mooney wrong in two ways: most Cherokees who can read and write Cherokee today are familiar with some version of phonetic spelling using the roman alphabet as well as with the syllabary. The syllabary has not fallen into disuse; it has been supplemented by additional systems for writing Cherokee. Mooney's implicit suggestion that monolingual Cherokees were a phenomenon of the past was also premature. There were monolingual Cherokees in North Carolina as late as the 1930s (Gilbert 1978), and possibly later, and there are still elderly speakers today who feel more comfortable using Cherokee than English.

The two trends that Mooney is reporting do ring true—a simultaneous love for the syllabary as a source of Indianness and an alienation from it on the part of the mixed-blood, English-speaking elite both surely existed at the time of his research. Instead of these trends resulting in the disappearance of the syllabary, however, they have somehow fused so that the syllabary has been retained as a symbolic source of identity alongside phonetic spellings that are accessible to marginal or nonspeakers of Cherokee.

Mooney's prediction that syllabic writing of Cherokee would be completely replaced by writing in English did not take into account the language education and cultural revitalization that is now taking place. A love of and pride in the syllabary exist side by side with a preference in some contexts for phonetic spelling.

Chapter Two

Reading, Writing, and the Reproduction of Cultural Categories

Three R's of Orthographic Choice in Cherokee Language Education

*T*his is the first of four chapters in which I describe the various types of syllabary usage I observed in the Eastern Cherokee community in the mid-1990s. I argue that the syllabary is treated as a kind of "code." Of course, all writing systems encode spoken language, but here I mean something a bit more metaphorical, along the lines of a cryptographic system. The concept of syllabary as code helps to reveal the coherence of a set of beliefs, behaviors, and material products, including literacy practices and performances—reading, writing, possessing, and wearing materials in syllabary; literacy learning and teaching practices in syllabary; and the perceived nature of syllabic texts of various forms.

This notion that the syllabary is treated as a code is suggestive in several ways. The word "code" connotes exclusion, and since the syllabary was developed for writing the Cherokee language, one might presume that the exclusion is directed at English-speaking people, the English language, or both. The situation is rather more complex in reality. The syllabary plays a highly specialized role as one of four orthographies for writing Cherokee, and this complex inventory of orthographies rests squarely on a base of presumed English-language fluency and literacy.

Before trying to understand the roles played by the syllabary in contemporary Cherokee education and culture, it is necessary to get a wider perspective on Cherokee education and language use. The role of formal education in the life of the community overall, as well as the dominance of English in the local linguistic and educational environments, provides context crucial for understanding the special place of the syllabary.

Education and Language among the Eastern Band

The Cherokee tribal school system, which was taken over by the Eastern Band of Cherokee Indians from the Bureau of Indian Affairs in the early 1990s, consists of an elementary, middle, and high school and serves the Cherokee population living on and near the reservation. Some Native American children from other tribal backgrounds, as well as some non-Indian children, mostly children of school staff, attend as well. Cherokee children have the choice of attending these schools or local public schools. I have been told that many Cherokee parents see the local public schools as providing a broader education, while the Cherokee schools provide more emphasis on Cherokee culture and language and a more comfortable learning environment because of the largely Cherokee population (see also Hipps 1994). Parents may choose which school to send their children to depending on which of these factors is most important to them, or for other reasons.

According to the 1990 census, 63.2 percent of Native Americans eighteen years and older living on the reserve were at least high school graduates; 1.4 percent of those between the ages of eighteen and twenty-four and 3.8 percent of those twenty-five and over had at least a bachelor's degree. Educational attainment seemed to differ somewhat for males and females, with 76.3 percent of males aged twenty-five to thirty-four having at least a high school diploma and 4.3 percent having at least a bachelor's degree, while the corresponding percentages for females were 80.3 and 9.3, respectively. The percentage of persons aged sixteen to nineteen who were not enrolled in school and not high school graduates was 22.1 in 1990 (U.S. Bureau of the Census 1990b: 65, 1061; Tables 14, 223). Educational attainment in the community seemed to increase considerably between 1980 and 1990. In 1980, the census indicated that 43.2 percent of persons twenty-five years and older were high school graduates, the corresponding percentage for 1990 being 63.1, and that 35.1 percent of persons aged sixteen to nineteen, as compared with 22.1 percent in 1990, were not enrolled in high school and not high school graduates (Reddy 1993: 425).

In 1990, 16.9 percent of Native Americans living on the reserve reportedly spoke a language other than English at home. Presumably, in almost all cases, this language was Cherokee. Reportedly, 4.7 percent also did not speak English "very well," and there were fifty linguistically isolated households (U.S. Bureau of the Census 1990b: 65, 1061; Tables 14, 223).[1]

Reading and Writing in English

My experience in Cherokee, North Carolina, suggested that there was a wide range of ability and practice among members of the community with regard to the reading and writing of English. The people I came to know included at least one who did not read or write in English at all, as well as several who had graduate degrees. One friend was responsible for writing and reviewing tribal grant applications. Another acquaintance could not get enough to read about politics and history and made frequent trips to the local university library. Nearly all homes I visited contained frequently read English Bibles as well as other church literature.

Nearly everyone I knew in Cherokee faithfully read the *Cherokee One Feather,* the local English-language newspaper, to get news of current tribal politics, deaths, gospel sings, yard sales, and other local events. In 1995 during the off-season, when few copies were going to tourists, the paper had a circulation of twenty-seven hundred, which averages out to be considerably more than one per household. U.S. census figures listed the number of households on the reservation as 1,786 in 1990 (U.S. Bureau of the Census 1990a: 90, Table 15). The front page of a sample issue (16 August 1995) contained the following headlines: "August 3 & 4 Council Report," "Casino Site Negotiations Reach Final Stage," "Principal Chief's Report to the People," "Magic Waters Site Chosen for Casino," "Meeting for Miss Cherokee/Miss Fall Festival Contestants," and "Fan Bus to Braves Football Game at Enka." Despite some attempts to integrate Cherokee language material into the paper, discussed in detail below, it has remained overwhelmingly an English-language publication.

One of the *One Feather*'s most important functions was partly taken over by television when Cherokee Cablevision began broadcasting the Cherokee tribal council meetings live. Watching these proceedings (which, in my experience, nearly everyone does, at home or in the workplace) has become an alternative to reading the summary of resolutions passed, tabled, and killed that appears each month in the paper.

A local postmaster estimated that 99 percent of writing on the Boundary was done in English. This community member, who is a fluent reader, writer, and speaker of Cherokee, had received only three personal letters written in Cherokee in forty years. During World War II, he told me, correspondence in the syllabary was more common, and parents and sons sometimes kept in touch this way.

He drew on his experience as postmaster to tell me about common types of reading on the reservation. A great number of magazines passed through the post office, he said, as well as considerable "junk" bulk mailings. Among the most popular periodicals were sports magazines, women's magazines like *Ladies Home Journal*, religious periodicals, particularly the recipient's denominational paper (although these were declining in popularity), and *National Geographic*. He believed that the education level of postal customers in Cherokee had more to do with the type of reading material they received in the mail than did their "traditionalism" or degree of Indian blood. Personal letters were becoming less common, as was true everywhere, he said, and mail was largely made up of bills. He noted that many people on the reservation, especially the elderly, responded to bills not by writing checks and mailing them back but by paying in person with cash. My experience confirms this.

An Eastern Band member who served as liaison between the community and a local educational institution gave me her general impressions of reading and writing in the community. She noted that since her institution communicated with adults in the community by means of written notices and since she got a good response to (and was frequently questioned about) these notices, it was fair to assume that at least this type of reading was being done at a fairly steady level in the community. She reiterated that nearly everyone in the community read the *Cherokee One Feather* and that they were particularly doing so at the time of our interview, to keep up on political "gossip." Home Bible study in English was very common, she said. Because of a lack of local diversions, novels and magazines were popular sources of entertainment, even among young kids. She noted that when magazine subscriptions were sold as a fund-raising event for her institution, they "raked in a lot!"

A staff member at the tribal high school told me that high school students received a good hour to hour and a half of homework each night and that middle school students received at least some homework each night. This staff member reported that there were few complaints about this amount of homework, suggesting that parents supported the work their children were doing. According to this source, students at all levels in the combined middle and high school spent a good part of their day, approximately 75–80 percent, reading and writing.

An elementary school administrator painted a somewhat different picture. This administrator argued that low levels of parental involvement, along with family bilingualism, affected reading levels at the school.[2] Some parents may have been intimidated by the school environment, the administrator said, especially if they themselves did not finish school.

This school representative went on to say, however, that while in school the students spent all of their morning hours, a three-hour block, on language arts, which were especially emphasized in grades one through three. The library and Cherokee culture and language staff, she said, encouraged the classroom teachers to select reading materials such as Native American literature. Native American myths were particularly popular. A program at the elementary school called the 50 Book Club, in which students receive a T-shirt bearing English and syllabic writing in Cherokee when they have read fifty books, encouraged reading. Students received thirty or forty minutes of homework per night in the upper grades and an average of ten minutes per night in grades one through three, according to the same administrator.

Other local institutions besides the tribal school system supported the reading and writing of English. Both the local community college and the local university had centers in Cherokee, the former offering courses in basic skills, including adult basic education (literacy) and GED (high school equivalency). Of the 1,079 students served by the local community college during the 1992–93 school year in these classes, 104 were Native American. The great majority of these students were enrolled in adult basic education classes and slightly more than half were between the ages of sixteen and twenty-four. Approximately 90 percent of these students were between the ages of sixteen and forty-four. Men and women participated about equally in these classes; forty-nine students were male and fifty-five were female (Kathryn Z. Forbes, pers. com., March 1995).

One tribal school staff member told me that the local community college had begun offering adult basic education classes in one of the local communities, rather than in downtown Cherokee. This class, she said, had a healthy membership of ten or twelve people the first time it was offered. She expected the class to succeed because it was taught by an Indian instructor and was taught in the local community.

There is also a public library on the reservation. The library was usually busy when I was there, perhaps in part because of its central and prominent location in the community's civic center. This civic center is also the site of day care programs, after-school programs, and many community social events.

The following data come from the annual report given by the library to the tribal council for the fiscal year 1993–94:

- Their door count, 8,434, was a slight increase from the previous year.
- That year 6,908 nonfiction, 972 adult fiction, and 1,816 children's books had been checked out.
- The children's section was busier than during the previous year because of participants in the 50 Book Club at Cherokee Elementary School.
- In the library 1,034 books were used.
- The above included parents reading to children, people looking at genealogical materials, students conducting research, and people seeking recipes.
- In the library 863 people read magazines for enjoyment.
- The library issued 73 library cards that year, making the total number 4,926.
- The library hosted several local meetings, including the community college's orientation class and the Quiz Bowl.
- In addition to several mainstream magazines such as *Glamour* and

Motor Trend, the library featured such periodicals as the *Journal of Cherokee Studies* and *Whispering Wind.*

- Native American newspapers carried included *Akwesasne Notes,* the *Indian Trader,* the *Seminole Tribune,* the *Cherokee Advocate,* and the *Cherokee One Feather.*
- Leftover magazines were donated to local institutions such as the senior citizens' center, the Cherokee Children's Home, the local branch of Job Corps, a local church day care, and the elementary school's art department.
- That year 984 people from twenty-nine U.S. states and Canada came to the library to do genealogical research.

In addition to this public library, there were more specialized archives containing documents and other material related to Cherokee language, culture, and history, located above the tribal museum. According to the archivist who worked at the museum in 1995, the archives served a wide range of clients, including Cherokee and non-Cherokee students from the local university, local high schools, and Robbinsville High School (which served the Snowbird Community), Cherokee and non-Cherokee scholars, local Cherokee quilt makers looking for traditional patterns, and Cherokees just wanting to browse.

Another source of written English-language materials on the Boundary was a local free book distribution center run by a prominent, long-time resident of the Boundary. This center, now closed, distributed free books to community members and local educators and was usually busy when open. In 1993, having been open for ten years, the center gave away its 1,250,000th book.

There was a noticeable asymmetry in the distribution of English-language materials in the outdoor visual landscape of Cherokee in the mid-1990s. The downtown and main routes in and out were plastered with English-language advertisements and directional signs. Concentrated in the downtown area were large official brown signs with white lettering, giving the names and locations of prominent businesses and attractions, mounted between enormous arrows. Some business signs were lit up, and some had interesting shapes such as a fish, an eagle, or an arrow. Stylized "Indian" arrows were probably the most common accompaniment to lettering on the signs, pointing toward a business or attraction's location and at the same time "Indianizing" it. Some signs featured neon lettering or a neon arrow. At the entrance points to the reservation, small green official signs marked the boundary, but these points were also marked by huge, decorative wooden signs. Hand-written signs, very rare, seemed to be either personal ("no U-turn") or political ("no dumps on the reservation"). The frequent signs desig-nating churches tended to be brown or wooden, not white, and never neon. As one got farther from downtown, the signs became less flashy and few and far between. A local project to standardize street signs and rename streets distributed signs in parts of the reservation that previously had few road signs.

A tribal council resolution passed in 1994 required that some of the shops in Cherokee change their prominently displayed names because they were considered to be derogatory or disrespectful to the Indian community. Store names that had to go included the Honest Injun and the Buck and Squaw.

There were few bulletin boards, downtown or elsewhere, contain-ing advertisements or notices of events. News of this sort seemed to spread by word of mouth or through the paper rather than the distri-bution of flyers. Cherokee Cablevision also flashed announcements of events in English.

Reading and Writing in Cherokee

In the 1970s, a bilingual education program was started at the tribal schools. One of the goals of this program was to teach children the Cherokee syllabary, and in the process of setting up the program, some of the teachers learned the syllabary. Some of the people trained in this program number among the major teachers of Cherokee culture and language, as well as producers of artifacts in the syllabary, on the reser-vation today. One of my consultants described the learning experience in the following way:

> The first contact I had with [the syllabary] was when I worked with the bilingual program. That was in 1977, and I was resource specialist in Cherokee history at the time, but along with teach-ing Cherokee history the first year, we also, to—get our kids to start using Cherokee language, when we made games and stuff we'd use the syllabary.

But we all basically learned to at least—even I, even though I wasn't in daily use of it, I learned some of it then.

But to really learn to write it, it wasn't 'til I came here, three years ago, and then along with teaching kids to write it, and they wrote things down and you had to help 'em every day for a week, you learned it, too. And that's really where I picked it up.

A teacher of a local syllabary course for adults said:

It was around the late 70s, when this bilingual project came into the high school system, and they needed people to teach the Cherokee language, and I thought that was a good time for me to share what I knew. I've always wanted to share the language with the younger generation, so I thought, well, this is the opportune time. So I applied, and I was one of the ones that got the position, to help teach the language. And there were about five of us, and I don't think any of us really knew how to read and write the Cherokee syllabary, so we all had to take some time and really get acquainted with it, and try to learn it in about two weeks' time.

So we all went to work at it. And . . . we just did it on our own. We all learned together. I mean, we had a chart, a syllabary chart, and I just studied it on my own, learned it on my own.

The future language teachers also received grammar lessons at that time from a non-Indian linguist.

The bilingual program ended after a few years, but in the late 1980s language classes were reintroduced in kindergarten through grade two. Subsequently, the offerings were expanded. In the mid-1990s, children were exposed to and taught the syllabary from kindergarten through high school, and adult classes emphasizing the syllabary were also available through the local university and community college. At all levels, the classes offered students alternative means of writing Cherokee as well, presenting one of several commonly used "phonetic"[3] systems. In the schools, and particularly in the elementary school, the syllabary was highly visible, from colorful signs bearing greetings and other phrases to a mural of Sequoyah holding a syllabary chart. The schools were also a major point of origin for syllabary-bearing artifacts that ultimately wound up in homes and as personal property. The schools produce various syllabary T-shirts each year, and in Cherokee language classes students produced items to be taken home such as greeting cards. These various educational uses of the syllabary are discussed in more detail below.

But other institutions, particularly local churches, have more consistently served as loci for the usage and visibility of the Cherokee syllabary. In the mid-1990s, several churches had special Sunday school classes in which the Bible was read in Cherokee, in syllabary. Even more common than the Cherokee New Testament, all syllabary, was the Cherokee songbook or hymnal, a pocket-sized, all-syllabary book carried around faithfully by most of the elderly Cherokees I knew. A local Methodist church printed the hymn "Amazing Grace" in Cherokee, using an alternative phonetic system, in its bulletin every week. This church's outdoor sign also contained Cherokee written using the same system.

In general, syllabary signs on the Boundary were few, although I was told that there were more in the years before my arrival. Many of the tribal buildings, generally out of the view of tourists, bore signs written in both syllabary and English, and the tribal elementary school was identified in syllabary on its front door. The syllabary sign that was most visible to tourists until recently was the neon sign for a downtown eatery, the Sequoyah Cafeteria (Figure 3).

If one ventured into the shops downtown, one would find syllabary in some form in nearly all of them. Most shops sold, at the very least, mugs, key rings, and postcards bearing the syllabary, arranged in the conventional chart. Others sold pieces of mock parchment, bearing the Lord's Prayer or a hymn in syllabary. Some sold pottery with syllabary designs. Others sold language books that actually taught the syllabary.

The annual Fall Festival, a homecoming for Cherokees but also an event that attracts tourists, tends to be a source of visible syllabary writing, with many displays of crafts, plants, food, and the like labeled in syllabary and with many artistic creations bearing the syllabary as a design. Some community displays nearly always include the Cherokee New Testament and other evidence of syllabary reading or writing in the community. The hall at the tribal ceremonial grounds, in which the displays at the Fall Festival were housed in the mid-1990s, also contained masks symbolizing each of the seven traditional Cherokee clans. These clan names were spelled out in the syllabary.

Figure 3. Neon syllabary-decorated sign for a downtown Cherokee business, no longer in operation. (Photograph by Frederic Gleach)

Some attempts were made to integrate Cherokee language material, and particularly material in the syllabary, into the *Cherokee One Feather* while I was in Cherokee. Many tribal offices, including that of the newspaper, purchased a computer program that allowed one to transform phonetic spellings of Cherokee words into the syllabic characters. Apparently, the paper had submitted a grant proposal, around the same time that it obtained this computer program, seeking support that would enable it to become fully bilingual. The bid was not successful, however, and the paper remained basically monolingual in English.

Many of the homes I visited in Cherokee contained syllabary charts, and nearly all, especially those of older Cherokees, contained the Cherokee New Testament and hymnal. In one home, a mother had put syllabary labels on household items and utilities for her children. I saw one license plate (the unofficial front one) in syllabary.

Syllabary makes its way to unexpected places, too. Right in downtown Franklin, North Carolina (approximately forty-five minutes south of Cherokee), there is an earthen mound, similar to others found throughout the area, called Nikwasi Mound. Next to the mound was an insurance company, called, logically enough, Indian Mound Insurance. The sign for this company also had a border designed with what appeared to be hand-fashioned syllabary characters. Some of these characters were hard to decipher (i.e., to match to one of the actual Sequoyan characters), and the writing on the sign appeared to have no meaning.

In downtown Asheville, North Carolina, approximately fifty miles east of Cherokee, I one day noticed several posters bearing syllabary characters on a billboard. The posters seemed to be part of a display celebrating Indigenous People's Day. There were pages from one of the most popular Cherokee language books containing syllabary, phonetics, and English up on the billboard. There were also pages from one of Sequoyah's biographies and a syllabary chart. I do not know the source, but near the top of the display there was a slogan, in syllabary, phonetics, and English: "ᏘᏌᏴ! *i-tsi-ye-gi!* Wake up!" This slogan (in Cherokee and English) was also used by an alternative political newsletter that was started up by a Big Cove resident while I was in the field.

The syllabary was clearly a key component of the semiotic landscape of the Boundary and its environs. It played a role in education, the media, tourism, religion, political activism—in every important dimension of Eastern Cherokee life.

Reading and Writing in Cherokee Language Education for Children

In the mid-1990s, many members of the Eastern Band were actively seeking to preserve the Cherokee language, both as a living language and for posterity. A movement was under way to increase the amount of Cherokee language instruction in the Cherokee tribal schools at all levels; the stated goal was to increase the fluency of graduating seniors from Cherokee High School. In an attempt to improve the amount and quality of resource materials available to teachers, one elementary school teacher initiated and then directed a language preservation and education project. This was initially a grant-funded project with ties to the Cherokee Central Schools, but the Eastern Band subsequently took responsibility for and funded the project. Its goals in the mid-1990s included the production of a Cherokee talking dictionary, a series of grammar lessons, and a series of bilingual videotapes of Cherokee elders. These efforts received support from many community members and from the tribal council and school board.

During the same period, the syllabary was increasingly visible in Cherokee artwork, at the Cherokee Fall Festival, in school hallways, on T-shirts—in general, in the local semiotic landscape.

These two trends would seem to go together logically; it makes sense that if interest in the Cherokee language was increasing, interest in its native-developed writing system would increase at the same time. If the two trends were related, however, they were not necessarily one and the same. For while the visible presence of the syllabary in a wide range of contexts served as a vehicle for Cherokee self-representation and the expression of pride, it was not treated as the most appropriate writing system to use in the teaching or preservation of the Cherokee language. In the pages ahead, I will consider the role played by the syllabary in two of the Cherokee tribal schools' language classrooms and in one local public school's Cherokee language class, paying particular attention to the presuppositions about the syl-

labary's nature as a writing system that were evident when the syllabary was taught and used. My observations in this section are based
largely on one semester of classroom observations in the tribal and
public schools, conducted during the spring of 1994, as well as on my
more general experience of being in the field for two and a half years
and maintaining contact with the Cherokee language instructors.

Although the availability of Cherokee language education is considered to be one of the biggest differences between the tribal and
public schools, the demands of the general curriculum were such that
not much time was available for it in the children's schedules in the
tribal schools. The amount of time increased as the children got older
so that by middle school they attended Cherokee language class for
two or three hours a week, while in the first grade they attended for
approximately twenty-five minutes per week. In high school, the language class was an elective. The language teachers were expected to
include cultural and historical material with their language lessons.

The public elementary school I visited was situated near the Qualla
Boundary, and its predominantly non-Indian student body included
some Cherokee children. The language class I observed was an elective; to attend it, students had to miss another special activity in which
the rest of their class was participating. Most students taking the class
were Cherokee. These classes met several times a week but only for a
few weeks at a time. Each class for fourth, fifth, or sixth graders was
approximately an hour long. As in the tribal schools, this instructor
included some Cherokee cultural material in his lessons such as films
on Cherokee culture and storytelling in English.

The Cherokee language instructors, in all the classrooms I observed,
clearly had much to do besides teach the Cherokee syllabary. But this
native writing system competed not only with other course material
but also with other systems for writing Cherokee. Children were introduced from the beginning to a conventional way of writing Cherokee
described by most teachers as "phonetic." The consonants have values
roughly equivalent to those in English in this system, but the vowels
have values that must be learned, what are sometimes called the "Continental" values. In this system, ⟨a⟩ stands for /a/, ⟨e⟩ for /e/, and so
on. This system, which I will refer to as the "standard phonetics," is reflected in the phonetic values on the syllabary chart, still in use today,

that was popularized by Samuel Worcester in the pages of the *Chero-kee Phoenix* in 1828.[4] This system may also be considered "standard" because, as with the syllabary itself, spellings do not change to reflect the speaker's local dialect—it is understood that the standard phonetic spelling ⟨tsa⟩ may be pronounced in a variety of ways, for example as [tsa] or [tsha], [tʃa] or [tʃha], depending on the speaker's dialect and the context in which it occurs.[5] Thus pronunciations of the written word ⟨Tsalagi⟩, 'Cherokee,' may sound to a native speaker of English like a word spelled "Tzalagi" or "Jalagi" depending on, for example, whether the Cherokee speaker is from the Qualla Boundary or from Snowbird.

Looking Like Cherokee: The Visibility of the Syllabary

In the tribal schools in the mid-1990s, children were expected to learn to read and write in this phonetic system beginning in the early grades, whereas they were not expected to start working regularly with the syllabary until the fourth grade. Still, children of all grades were constantly exposed to the syllabary visually.

A syllabary chart adorned the wall of nearly every classroom in Cherokee Elementary School. Colorful paper signs contained messages such as ⟨ᏏᏲ⟩ (*siyo*), 'hello,' written in the syllabary on many classroom doors. A large mural of Sequoyah holding a syllabary chart decorated a central hallway. The details of this chart did not match the commonly reproduced versions of the syllabary; it was unnecessary to be that specific because the image of Sequoyah holding any writing surface marked with any subset of the syllabary's characters is iconic of the syllabary's invention and its existence as a complete system. Teachers' names were sometimes posted in syllabary. On my first visit to Cherokee Elementary School, I was briefly shown a large, colorful outdoor mural that illustrated the Cherokee myth according to which the animals of the world had to retrieve fire from a tree on an island on which it had been placed by the Thunderers, the two Cherokee creators. This mural was captioned in syllabary. Like the mythic scene in the mural itself and like the mural of Sequoyah, the syllabary generally served as an icon of Cherokee culture and identity, whether or not it was "read" in the conventional sense.

The syllabary was especially omnipresent in the elementary school's

Cherokee language classroom. Though the specific messages changed, on any given day the language classroom walls would boast several Cherokee messages, usually in syllabary and phonetics, on brightly colored paper. Throughout the school year, one wall contained pictures of animals, with their names in English, phonetics, and syllabary. A seasonal poster, illustrating the month with an appropriate image (such as a snowman for January) and the word for the month in English, standard phonetics, and syllabary, was featured on another wall. After the Christmas break a sign greeted children with the word "ՏᏣᏬWhᎤꙄ," with "Welcome back" written alongside. Most prominently, one wall held a large version of the traditional syllabary chart, black letters on white, surrounded by an eye-catching bright pink border.

Some signs and posters featured the syllabary by itself, without other accompanying writing. A glossy poster, celebrating Native North America Month (November 1993), contained "DBᎾꙄ" (*ayv:wiya*, 'Indian'), untranslated and untransliterated, in syllabary. Another sign, written by a teacher, read "ᏣᏪᎩ ᏗᏒᏣᏓᎤᏗ" (*tsalaki titehlokwasti hahni*, 'We learn Cherokee here'). This sentence, written as though uttered by students—'we learn'—would seem to represent the teachers' trying to will language learning into being. If students *could* read the sign, they *would* be learning Cherokee. The indexical relationship between the sign and the targeted student reader was similar to that established by the advertisement so frequently seen on buses and subways in New York City when I was growing up: "f u cn rd ths msj u cn gt a gd jb." Since students never seemed to decode or even acknowledge this sign, however, the indexical relationship between the sign and students was one teachers *hoped* would exist. The indexicality of the sign may have been functioning on other levels as well, for example, from the teachers to themselves, each other, parents, administrators, visitors, or students: we are the sort of teachers who have students—or strive to have students—who can read this syllabary-only sign. Another sign simply read "ᏲᎯ" (*siyo*, 'hello').

The blackboard was also an important source of syllabary, with the teacher frequently writing vocabulary words on the board in both syllabary and standard phonetics. Around Valentine's Day, the board contained

> E Ᏽ Ꮐ̃
> Gv ge yu
> I love you.

and also

> R Ᏺ T
> Mother = E-tsi-i

Almost throughout the duration of my visits, one corner of the classroom contained

> E-tla-we-i
> R Ꮑ ꮞ T

which means 'quiet.'[6] On other days, the board might contain the ubiquitous ⟨ᏣᎳᏫ⟩, with ⟨Tsa-la-gi⟩ and ⟨Cherokee⟩ written underneath.

The syllabary also appeared in the classroom on students' T-shirts, Cherokee language books, and some, though not many, of the class work sheets. Ironically, the work sheets most likely to contain syllabary were those given to the youngest children, those not yet responsible for learning the syllabary. For example, kindergarten students were given a handout almost completely filled with an image of a large hand. Starting with the thumb, the fingers were numbered, in syllabary, from one to five. The thumb was thus labeled "Ᏻꮢ" (*sa:kwu*, 'one'), the index finger "ᏪᎴ" (*tha?li*, 'two'), and so on. The handout contained no English or phonetic spellings, but each of the fingers was marked with stars in the same number that it was supposed to represent. The classroom also contained an all-syllabary clock. (See Figure 4 for an illustration of a syllabary clock face.) The elementary school classroom, then, was very richly marked with the syllabary, making it iconically and indexically the most Cherokee space in the school. It was both the most "Cherokee-looking," and the room that gave the most evidence of Cherokee-specific linguistic and cultural activity.

In the tribal middle school class I visited, the syllabary was less emphasized than in the tribal elementary school. Most students had, or

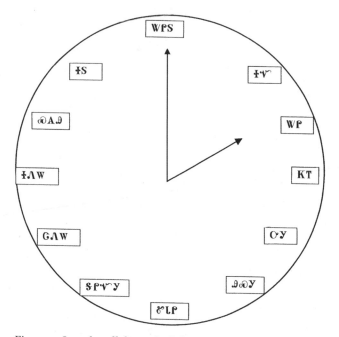

Figure 4. Sample syllabary clock face.

were given as needed, copies of the syllabary chart to use for assignments. Syllabary was not written on the blackboard, but students were expected to write it in assignments. Although there were Cherokee expressions written on the walls in the main hall shared by the middle and high schools, they were in phonetics, accompanied by a friendly reminder, "Cherokee—Use It or Lose It."

Because of their limited duration, the local public school classes I attended did not take place in a classroom permanently devoted to Cherokee language education. Therefore, the syllabary was not as visually present in the learning environment as it was in the tribal schools. This teacher did not write in syllabary on the board, put the syllabary on handouts, or expect students to learn the syllabary. But these students, unlike those at the tribal schools, used a popular Cherokee language book (Chiltoskey 1972) that contains each entry in syllabary as well as in standard phonetics.

Although it was present and used to varying degrees, then, the syllabary was visually present, in one way or another, in all these educational environments. Special care seemed to be taken to make the syllabary part of the semiotic landscape of children, even when they were not required to know or reproduce it. Even in the tribal elementary school, where it seemed that syllabary was most strongly emphasized, children were not required to use it until the fourth grade, and even then it was used in very specific ways that I will spell out shortly. Yet the impression remained that the syllabary was something adults wanted children of all ages to *see*.

A Plurality of Writing Systems

The process of integrating the teaching of the two writing systems I have discussed thus far, syllabary and standard phonetics, was complicated by the fact that the teachers displayed varying abilities and preferences with respect to use of the syllabary and even the standard phonetic system. Of the three teachers in Cherokee Elementary School's Cherokee language classroom, Teacher 1, a Qualla Boundary resident, used both syllabary and standard phonetics; Teacher 2, an Oklahoma Cherokee, mainly used the standard phonetics; and Teacher 3, a Snowbird resident, generally did not use either. The three teachers worked together as a team, with Teacher 1 writing both syllabary and phonetics on the board, Teacher 2 not doing much writing, and Teacher 3 sometimes putting his own phonetics up on the board—a system in which ⟨ah⟩ might stand for /a/, and other vowels might be written ⟨ay⟩, ⟨ee⟩, ⟨oe⟩, ⟨oo⟩, ⟨uh⟩, and in which the writing of some consonants was altered to reflect his own dialectal pronunciations. I call this type of spelling "easy" phonetics, since that is how it was most frequently characterized by users. (See Figure 5 for a comparison of Cherokee orthographies.) Teacher 3 advised the children to look at these spellings if they could not "understand" the standard phonetic system. For example, while the classes were studying the Cherokee words for colors, Teacher 3 put the following words on the board:

ah-jeh-e
oo-Neh-Gah
Gee-Gah-Geh
Sha-koe-Nee-Gay
Oo-woe-dee-geh
Dah-Lon-Nee-gey[7]

He called these the "real" phonetics, explaining that by reading these spellings students might be able to "see a little bit better" how the words are pronounced. By contrast, he said, the standard phonetic spellings are written according to the syllabary, which meant that they come from the syllabary chart. He thus implied that the historical association between standard phonetics and the syllabary makes standard phonetics difficult. The "easy" system used above spells the same syllable, /ke/, in three different ways—"Geh" (or "geh"), "Gay," and "gey." Yet it is doubtful that this would interfere with correct pronunciation because the spellings rest firmly on the presupposed English-language fluency and literacy of the students.

On another occasion, the elementary school students were asked to give *Good Morning America*'s namesake communal greeting on the air—and in Cherokee. The phrase was first translated literally into Cherokee by Teacher 2, as *o:sta sunale:ʔi amaye:hli*—literally 'good' 'morning' (not a customary Cherokee greeting) 'America.' He then explained that he had written the phrase out for the children's homeroom teachers in "English spelling" or "English phonetics," referring in this way to his version of "easy phonetics." Easy phonetics were thus seen by this teacher as being closer to English and at the same time more accessible than other ways of writing Cherokee. Conversely, standard phonetics, which we have seen to be linked with syllabary, were seen as being more Cherokee (certainly less "English") and also less accessible, at least to nonspeakers of Cherokee. It is important to understand that easy phonetics, which are described by their users as "easier to understand," or "easier to see," are considered to be the most transparent. That is, they are seen as the form of writing most transparently connected with spoken language, spoken Cherokee in particular. To nonspeakers of English, of course, "easy phonetics" would not appear "easy" or transparent. Thus a generally unconscious presupposition of English-language literacy underlies this hierarchy of systems that is elided in the very process of its perpetuation. The English-language hegemony underlying this hierarchy is made invisible by the position of neutrality or transparency in which the easy phonetics are placed by the writing hierarchy.

The Cherokee Middle School teacher whose class I visited was reluctant enough about the standard phonetics or felt the students would

Orthography			
International Phonetic Alphabet	"International" or "Linguist's" Phonetics (see Cook 1979)	"Standard" Phonetics	"Easy" or "Anglo" Phonetics
Consonants			
t	t	d	d
t^h	th or t^h	t	t
k	k	g	g
k^h	k^h or kh	k	k
k^w	k^w or kw	qu or gw	gw
k^{hw}	k^{hw} or khw	qu or kw	kw
ts	ts	ts	dz or j
ts^h	t^hs or ths	ts	ts or ch
ʔ	ʔ	ʔ or –	–
Vowels			
ɑ	a	a	ah, etc.
e	e	e	ay, eh, etc.
i	i	i	ee, etc.
o	o	o	oh, oe, etc.
u	u	u	oo, etc.
ə̃	v	v	uh, etc.

Figure 5. The four orthographies used in Eastern Cherokee language education. In addition to the differences highlighted in the figure, "international" phonetics records suprasegmentals such as stress and vowel length not reflected in the other orthographies. For example, the word for 'cucumber' would be *ka:kama* in "international" phonetics (and following Cook 1979), *gagama* in "standard" phonetics, and something like *gahgahmah* in "easy" phonetics.

find them difficult enough that he handed out a reference sheet for students, translating standard phonetics into easy phonetic values. In writing on the board, however, and on handouts, this teacher normally used standard phonetics with the slight modification of adding in the intrusive h. So, for example, instead of writing the word for 'my aunt' as ⟨a gi lo gi⟩, he wrote it as ⟨a gi hlo gi⟩. In addition, the standard ⟨s⟩ used to represent either [s] or [ʃ], depending on the speaker's dialect, was occasionally written ⟨sh⟩, as in the Cherokee word ⟨shu:li⟩, 'buzzard.'

In the public school classes I visited, the teacher frequently wrote on the board in easy phonetics. On one particular day, he wrote the date on the board as follows:

A-Nu-ye
So-Gwo
TA-Le-Ne-E-GA

He was representing, respectively, the words *anv:yi, so:kwo, thaline:ʔika,* 'March, 1, Tuesday.' Earlier, we saw an example of how there can be many different easy spellings for one phoneme or spoken syllable; here we see one easy representation standing for two phonemes. The letter ⟨e⟩ here was being used to represent both the vowels /i/ and /e/. The teacher explained to me that he was writing the date this way to make it easier on the children so they could "see it." The "e's" should be "i's," he said. "When I look at it, I can see it should be /i/." When not writing on the board himself, this teacher used the standard phonetic spellings found in *Cherokee Words* (Chiltoskey 1972). But the children were not expected to learn these spellings and were encouraged, in their notes, to use their own easy system.

Yet another system of phonetic writing, one that closely resembles systems used by linguists to write Cherokee and other Iroquoian languages, occasionally made its way into the classrooms as well. This system, preferred by at least one teacher, differs from the standard phonetic system in its writing of some consonants and in that the glottal stop, vowel length, pitch, and intrusive h, omitted from the standard phonetic writing, are all recorded. The Eastern Cherokee Language Project, which has a history of contact with linguists, developed quite a bit of material in this system for use in classrooms in the 1990s. I will refer to this system as "international" phonetics because that is how it was referred to by those language teachers who used a specific name for it. This name presumably came from the system's similarity to the International Phonetic Alphabet. It might also be called "linguist's" phonetics. This system, though it is clearly intended as a relatively more narrow means of transcription than either the syllabary or the other phonetic systems, is seen by many as being difficult and inaccessible, like the syllabary itself. In particular, language teachers complain (or report that their students complain) about the use of ⟨k⟩ and ⟨t⟩ for /k/ and /t/. Teacher 3 particularly objected to the use of ⟨th⟩ to represent /th/. The diagraph ⟨th⟩, he told me, stands for the first sounds in "this, that, and Thatcher!" He considered the use of ⟨kw⟩ and ⟨khw⟩ as contrasted with the ⟨qu⟩ spellings on the syllabary chart to be "wrong" as well. I heard this objection from other speakers too and wonder whether ⟨q⟩ might be preferred because it resembles a ⟨g⟩ and thus is considered to represent the consonant more faithfully in those contexts in which it is voiced. This teacher's objections might also have arisen from the marginality of his own dialect from the point of view of the leaders of the language preservation project. Because he was from the relatively remote Snowbird community, his dialect was similar to the Cherokee spoken in Oklahoma and differed in important ways from that of most Qualla speakers.

In any case, the presence of these four writing systems (the syllabary, the standard phonetics, easy phonetics, and international phonetics) and the perceived need for teachers and students to move among them suggested a range of accessibility, with easy phonetics being most accessible (implicitly, to readers of English) and the syllabary being least accessible. This hierarchy obscures the fact that the syllabary is, by definition, a phonetic writing system—though it is, to be sure, a system for relatively broad transcription. It might be true, as the local ideology seems to hold, that it would be difficult for early primary school children to memorize the phonetic values of the eighty-five syllabic characters. But at the same time, it would probably not be much more obvious to most first graders that ⟨gv⟩, a standard phonetic spelling, should be pronounced /kv/ than that ⟨E⟩, the syllabic character for /kv/, should be pronounced /kv/. The presence of the easy phonetics implied that even the standard phonetics were not easily memorized, that they did not come easily to readers and writers of English. The syllabary then came to be seen as even more difficult and inaccessible. Possibly as a result of the presence of these easy phonetics, many students in the classes I visited were unable to pronounce Cherokee words correctly by reading the standard phonetics because they had not memorized the values of vowels. Whether they fared better with the easy phonetics depended on whether they were of sufficient age to have absorbed English spelling patterns to the point that they seemed neutral and transparent. Teachers also sometimes reinforced the apparent difficulty of the standard phonetics. In one example, a teacher wrote the Cherokee word for 'and,' ⟨no-le⟩, on the blackboard. Without any student expressing difficulty, he jumped in to explain, "This word is a little hard to read; it looks like 'knoll' but it's really *no-le*."

Some language educators argued that the syllabary is more difficult than phonetic writing because it does not completely represent the sounds of Cherokee. It omits the glottal stop, intrusive h, vowel length, and pitch, all of which can substantially change the pronunciation and meaning of words. But the standard phonetic system used in most classes makes exactly these same omissions. In fact, the phonetic syllables used have a direct one-to-one correspondence with the syllabary characters as represented by the chart. In addition, all of the orthographies except the international phonetic system were used so as to reflect syllable breaks as they would be defined by the syllabary. Even when the syllabary was not used, then, its structure shaped the patterns of written Cherokee.

In this context, it should not be surprising to learn that the children did not generally read the Cherokee words to learn how to say them. Rather, they listened to the teacher and then matched the pronunciation they heard with the spelling or a set of spelling variants. Rather than reading Cherokee words to get information about how to pronounce them, as students might be encouraged to do in reading English, students in the Cherokee language classes learned pronunciation by listening to and mimicking their teachers. Words spelled in whatever system were then associated, contextually, with the spoken word. In short, they seemed to learn the Cherokee words as sight words regardless of which writing system was used.

But it may not be quite true that the children learned these words as sight words because it was not always clear that they were focusing on written words at all, and therefore the appearance of words seemed to be largely irrelevant. Students in all classes did most of their pronouncing of Cherokee words in the context of repeating what teachers said, even when a given teacher's pronunciation was noticeably different from what seemed to be written. For example, when a standard phonetic spelling ⟨o si gwo tsu⟩ was on the board and a teacher's pronunciation of the same word was /ohsi:kwu:tsv/, students would routinely repeat the teacher's pronunciation. (In this particular case, which involved the pronunciation of a greeting meaning roughly 'how are you?' students were flexible, moving easily between pronunciations they may have heard locally or from another teacher and the one they heard in the classroom from this particular teacher.) When students did actually attempt to extract pronunciations from written words, they were by and large unsuccessful, particularly with respect to vowel pronunciation. There were occasional exceptions when students actually read (correctly) a different pronunciation than the one given by the teacher, but they were fairly rare.

The details of writing and reading, then, became largely irrelevant, except perhaps to provide students with general consonant-linked clues as to what word was intended. This led me to wonder why instructors did not start teaching the syllabary right away, in the early grades, and why the hierarchy of these (to some degree irrelevant) writing systems seemed so firmly upheld. The sharp contrast between syllabic and easy phonetic writing and the delay in learning the syllabary communicated two implicit messages: first, that the syllabary is not phonetic; and second, that it is difficult to use and learn.

Many additional associations of the syllabary emerged out of the functions it served when it was used in the classroom. One such association is related to a larger ideology of U.S. education, according to which writing is seen as something that children do not inherently want to do. In the middle school, writing sentences was sometimes used as punishment. In detention, students were sometimes required to look up and copy definitions. This pattern had made its way into the middle school Cherokee language classes, where students were told to write either in English or phonetic (and more Anglicized) Cherokee when they had misbehaved. I observed two students required to write ⟨to h(i) a gwa lo sdi⟩, 'I will sit still,' enough times to fill the front and back of a sheet of paper. But, and this is the important point, I *never* observed writing in the syllabary given as a punishment. Rather, it was offered in the middle school as extra credit for those who wanted it. Writing in the syllabary thus gained positive connotations, contrasted with the potentially negative connotations of the phonetic writing. In the elementary school, this special nature of the syllabary took the form of it being an *extra,* or *advanced,* category of writing. Even when fourth graders started writing the syllabary, it was nearly always in addition to, not instead of, phonetics.

This specialness is underscored by several other distinguishing features of the syllabary. For one, the syllabary was treated as if it were more designlike than phonetic writing or writing in English. The elementary school children were occasionally given coloring sheets bearing pictures and a Cherokee word in syllabary. The syllabary characters were outlined so that they could be colored in as well as the picture. I never saw the phonetic (romanized) Cherokee letters offered for coloring in this way. The elementary school walls displayed much more syllabary than did those of the high school, where, at the same time, there was less design and color in general. The way teachers wrote the syllabary on the board, posters, and handouts also reinforced the design characteristics of the characters. Writing of the syllabary was stylized and deliberate when compared with writing of phonetic Cherokee or English words. Flourishes were rarely omitted when writing the syllabary characters, even when they were not necessary for the character to be recognized.

This in turn may have had something to do with the fact that the syllabary was frequently copied, rather than written from memory. Part of the reason the teachers' writing of the syllabary was so stylized is that written syllabary in the classroom context seemed to be intended to look like printed syllabary. When the children began to write in syllabary in the fourth grade, what they really learned to do was to use the syllabary chart. They learned to look up phonetic values and translate them into syllabary characters, which they then copied. At the elementary and middle school levels, they were not expected to memorize the chart. They were thus not "writing" in the syllabary in the sense that one might expect but "copying" or transliterating. Generally speaking, then, the syllabary was not taught or learned as a handwriting system, as a script. What "writers" of syllabary in this context did, by and large, was reproduce print.

Possibly as a result of this pattern, there was relatively little creative or straightforwardly communicative use of the syllabary by students. In one classroom, a student had written various permutations of his name on the blackboard in English, over and over, and, amid it all, the syllabary character ⟨Ꮂ⟩ (/sa/) was written three times. This was one of the few examples of spontaneous syllabary use by a student that I witnessed, and it was not communicative in the straightforward sense— its usage, though potentially meaningful, did not seem to communicate a specific referential message.

A further difference between the connotations of the syllabary and those of the other writing systems in use at the schools is the syllabary's inalienable association with Cherokee language and culture. The students learned that the syllabary is *distinctly Cherokee*, not so much through lectures on its history as by means of the contexts in which it was most likely to appear. Students were familiar with the syllabary chart, which is intimately tied in with Cherokee history, since it is the same chart that was used by those who translated the New Testament into Cherokee and published the *Cherokee Phoenix*. The chart has also become a metonym for Sequoyah himself, since the two are nearly always depicted together in artwork. In my observations in the elementary school classroom, I noticed that the only time words were put up on the board in syllabary, without phonetics accompanying them, was when they were representing the four colors (blue, red, white, and black) traditionally associated in Cherokee culture with the cardinal directions. In the middle school, the exercise that most emphasized the syllabary was one on local place names, many of which are the names of Cherokee townships and some of which are also clan names. The syllabary was most likely to be called on as a writing medium, then, when the written content was seen as culturally Cherokee.

All of these associations of the syllabary—its opposition to phonetics, its being seen as difficult yet important for children to see, its being special in various ways (a source of extra credit and a supplemental type of writing, a source of beauty and design, a type of writing that is generally copied from an authoritative source, and, finally, a type of writing that is uniquely Cherokee)—point to the existence of a belief that writing in the syllabary is a different type of activity than writing in English or in romanized Cherokee.

When I put all of the features of the syllabary's usage that I observed in the classroom together, I was reminded of a teaching tool I used when I worked with second graders on reading and writing. We used

Figure 6. Type of "code" puzzle used to teach spelling in one Chicago elementary school.

handouts that contained codes of various kinds, requiring the children to fill in blanks or solve riddles by using codes, in which various shapes "stood for" letters of the alphabet (see Figure 6). Syllabary usage in the Cherokee tribal schools shared many features with our use of these codes: the shapes used in the codes were considered to be nonphonetic, they were primarily valuable as substitutes for another writing system that *was* phonetic, the codes had to be "cracked" and the phonetic values looked up in a chart or list, and the elements of the code were seen as being more designlike, being geometric or other shapes, than the letters for which they stood. If there is a unifying theme that links the various aspects of syllabary usage in the school system, it seems to be that the syllabary was functioning as a code. This theme is plausible not because of an analogy to my personal experience as a teacher but because of the strong reverberation of this concept of syllabary as code in other contexts of syllabary usage, as the reader will see in later chapters.

Note that codes are good not only for semiotic boundary-setting and for protecting knowledge but also for self-representation and identification. Part of this potential comes from the fact that in a code, the iconic (what it does or does not look like) and the indexical (what it suggests about writers, readers, and the texts produced in it) are foregrounded over the symbolic. The code functions only as a symbolic orthography for code-breakers—that is, for insiders.

Reading and Writing in the Adult Language Classroom

Cherokee and non-Cherokee adults in the community who wanted to learn to speak, read, or write Cherokee in a formal context had a variety of options while I was in Cherokee. The local university and community college, both of which have centers on the Boundary, offered Cherokee language classes for adults. Periodically, various churches in the area also offered classes, usually aimed at speakers who wanted to learn to read or write syllabary, rather than at nonspeakers.

I sat in on many of the adult classes during my time in Cherokee, learning a great deal from each of them. In the way syllabary was taught in these classes, I saw further evidence of the underlying cultural presuppositions of codelikeness that I have been describing above. The manifestations of these presuppositions differ from those seen in the children's classes, probably for several reasons: the students in these classes were adults, some of the classes had student populations that were racially and ethnically mixed, and some of them took place in specifically Christian contexts.

A hierarchy of writing systems, with the syllabary serving as the most prestigious and most culturally Cherokee system, could still be observed if one considered these classes as a group.

Adult Class A

The first class I attended was held at a higher educational institution, and the students were a mix of Cherokees and non-Cherokees. In this class, the teacher strove at first to use only syllabary, without any intervening phonetic writing. So, for example, this teacher taught us that ⟨R⟩ was pronounced /sv/ without giving us the phonetic spelling, and then gave an accompanying word, ⟨RY⟩ (/sv:ki/), 'onion,' also without phonetics, for us to learn. We were given assignments that asked us to match directly words in English with Cherokee words in syllabary. In addition, adults in this class were expected to learn the phonetic values of the characters by heart, and we were drilled on them frequently.

As the course progressed, however, the teacher did start using standard phonetics to accompany the syllabary. And from the very beginning, students were armed with the chart, giving them an ever-ready source of standard phonetic equivalents for the characters.

Even so, this class came close to treating the syllabary as a transparently phonetic system, probably because the teaching of syllabary, rather than general language proficiency, was the course's primary goal. It shared both of these features with the next class I attended.

Adult Class B

This class, mainly for speakers, was taught at a church by a local preacher. We were sometimes required to equate English words directly with Cherokee words in syllabary. For example, we would be supplied the English word "acorn" and asked to supply the Cherokee syllabary characters ⟨Jℰ⟩, /ku/ /le/. However, we were also expected to write syllabary characters in response to standard phonetic prompts. For example, we were expected to write ⟨S⟩ when prompted with ⟨ga⟩ and vice versa. Vocabulary words were given in syllabary and standard phonetics, as well as in English. This course was the only one in which I ever received a syllabary chart without accompanying phonetics.

Adult Class C

Another series of courses was taught at a higher educational institution, with a mix of Cherokee and non-Cherokee students. These classes varied in content and goals from one semester to the next so that the syllabary was sometimes taught and sometimes excluded. These courses also featured modified international phonetics in some semesters, and standard phonetics in others. In semesters when the modified international phonetics were being used, the Cherokee word for 'I am eating (an object)' was spelled ⟨tsiki?a⟩ with ⟨k⟩ representing /k/, and with the glottal stop represented. In other semesters, when modified standard phonetics were used, the same word would be written ⟨tsigi?a⟩. The exclusion of the syllabary from some semesters suggests that the syllabary was not necessarily seen as the inevitable system for writing and reading Cherokee, as an integral part of the language itself. Generally speaking, the syllabary was taught as an object in and of itself, and although students did progress to the point of writing sentences and compositions in the syllabary during semesters in which the syllabary was taught, requiring them simultaneously to possess knowledge of vocabulary and grammar as well as syllabary competency, syllabary was not the primary vehicle for teaching vocabulary or grammar.

Adult Class D

The final two adult classes I attended both relied heavily on the usage of easy phonetics. One was taught at a local higher educational institution, consisted mainly of non-Cherokees, and was led by a teacher from Oklahoma. This teacher did not use syllabary or standard phonetics and did not write at all—no work was done on the board nor handouts generated. Students were expected to take notes on the vocabulary taught, however, in whatever orthography we saw fit. The occasional suggestions made by the teacher as to how to spell a particular word clearly suggested an easy phonetic model. When I borrowed notes from my classmates, they contained spellings such as the following: "Do-he-u-de-cleg-co-heg" for *tohi:?udihlek kohi:k,* 'it's very hot today.' Significantly, this was the only adult class that contained no Christian content—we did not study hymns, biblical passages, or even any Christian vocabulary—and it was the only one that never approached the syllabary or used standard phonetics.

Adult Class E

The last adult class was taught by an Eastern Cherokee speaker at a higher educational institution, with a mix of Cherokee and non-Cherokee students. This teacher also relied heavily on easy phonetics, reserving syllabary almost exclusively for the contexts of Bible reading and hymn learning. Standard phonetics occurred as direct transliterational equivalents for syllabary characters and in handouts obtained from an Oklahoma source (not produced by the teacher). International phonetics occurred in additional handouts not generated by the teacher, possibly originating from the Eastern Cherokee Language Project or from some earlier collaboration between linguists and speakers. As in the children's classrooms, here the standard phonetics were treated as an intermediate step in making syllabic writing accessible to the student. The use of three lines of writing on a handout distributed by the teacher to teach us the Cherokee hymn sung to the tune "Amazing Grace" is a good illustration. Each line of the song was represented first in syllabary, as one would find it in the Cherokee hymnal, then in standard phonetics (the equivalents for each of the syllabary characters were we to look them up on the chart), and then in easy phonetics. For example, the first word, *une:hlanv:hi,* 'the creator,' usually translated as 'God,' was written

Ꭴ	Ꮑ	Ꮃ	Ꮕ	Ꭾ
u	ne	la	nv	hi
ooo-	nAy-	la-	nu-	he

Occasionally, the easy phonetics would be supplanted by a rebuslike substitution of a letter, whose name approximates a given phonetic syllable, for the syllable itself. Note, for example, the easy spelling of the last syllable in this word, *uwe:tsi,* 'his son':

Ꭴ	Ꮽ	Ꮵ
u	we	tsi
ooo-	way-	z

and the penultimate syllable in this word, *une:tseʔi,* 'he said':

Ꭴ	Ꮑ	Ꮴ	Ꭲ
u	ne	tse	i
ooo-	nay-	j-	e

Like the easy spellings more generally, these rebuslike substitutions also rest on a foundation of assumed American English–language literacy. That is, the names for these letters as given in American English must come naturally (they must read transparently) to the reader for this system to work.

*   *   *

CONSIDERING THESE FIVE ADULT CLASSES as a group, then, we see the full range of writing systems in use that were present in the school system's Cherokee language education program. The hierarchical arrangement of these systems, with the syllabary as the most prestigious and least phonetic system, was probably most visible in Class E, where that teacher used all of them. That class will be explored in more detail below, but for now it is worth noting that the classes in which the syllabary was treated as most phonetic were those in which teaching syllabary was the primary, or only, goal.

In the classes that were primarily syllabary literacy classes, the inaccessibility of the syllabary and its status as a code as described above may have seemed irrelevant. In these classes, some of the codelike features (such as treating the syllabary as nonphonetic, inaccessible, and a stand-in for phonetic systems) did not emerge strongly.

Teacher A, whose class was mainly for nonspeakers, may have seen teaching other aspects of the language as unrealistic or simply as beyond the scope of a beginning class. But in any event, the teaching of the syllabary did not coincide with the necessary cultural context to make the code powerful. In other words, if the learners of the syllabary were probably not going to learn Cherokee anyway (many were non-Indians), the syllabary's special place in the range of potential writing systems was not crucial to emphasize.

Teacher B was teaching fluent speakers, whose only need was to learn how to read and write syllabary. In this class, knowledge of the code coincided not only with fluent knowledge of Cherokee but also with a learning context that suggested appropriate intentionality. It is precisely in the context of Cherokee New Testament reading that total transparency, phonetic and semantic, was attributed to the syllabary by many of my consultants. Indeed, the syllabary New Testament was considered by many users to be their clearest point of access to the word of God—word in a superlinguistic sense. Some consultants suggested to me that the words in the syllabary New Testament cannot be changed, to reflect dialect in reading aloud, for example. The New Testament is held by many not just to provide access to a particular set of recorded spoken language, or a particular set of meanings, but to truth itself.

In Teacher A's predominantly nonspeaking class, the syllabary's link to the rest of the Cherokee language was very nearly severed because of the very limited usage expected of students. In the case of Class B, its link was very nearly irrelevant because of the syllabary's presupposed total (even nonlinguistic) transparency in the context of Bible reading, which users in that class were approaching. The syllabary functions as a protective code, but what it protects is not really some knowledge distinct from itself but its own meaningful usage. The syllabary did not need to serve this purpose in Teacher A's class because the class was not really providing a point of access to the rest of Cherokee language or to functional, communicative syllabary use—particularly writing.

The lexical associations of the syllabary in these various adult classes lend insight into the semantic parameters taught concurrently with the syllabary. As in the children's classes, syllabary tended to be strongly associated with certain topics. In the adult classes, the topics tended to be either Christian (specifically, the actual texts of the Cherokee New Testament or hymnal) or related in some way to the cultural and natural environments of the community. Names of local plants, animals, persons, communities, kin types, and culturally relevant activities such as weaving were popular vocabulary words.[8] The second type of semantic association may be seen as similar to the linkage in the children's language classrooms of syllabary with topics considered to be culturally Cherokee.[9] In Class C, the association between syllabic writing and the "natural" objects in the Cherokee environment was seen as being so strong that the teacher proposed that students collaborate on the production of a syllabary coloring book, featuring local plant and animal words, based on our lessons.

The prominence of biblical material in adult Cherokee language education represents a departure, however, and one that sheds new light on our understanding of the syllabary as code. The strong association between the syllabary and the Bible (and Christianity more broadly) is suggested by my observations that the Bible was used with beginners, for whom shorter, made-up phrases and sentences might be more appropriate from the language education point of view, and that alternatives (such as selections in syllabary from the Oklahoma publication the *Cherokee Advocate* or stories in the *Journal of Cherokee Studies*) were never used as representative texts. In one class, Psalm 121:1–2 (in syllabary) was distributed and students were expected to memorize it. In another, a prayer in syllabary was the only long syllabary text distributed. Teacher E used a Cherokee hymn, sung to the tune of "Amazing Grace," handwritten in syllabary, standard phonetics, and easy phonetics, in addition to direct readings from the Gospel of Matthew, in our learning of the syllabary. In this class, in which deciphering the New Testament was the teacher's primary purpose for working on the syllabary, reading proceeded through careful stages of decoding. As an assignment, we would be given a section of text and asked to find the standard phonetic value of each character. We were also encouraged to write down our own easy phonetic version of each syllable. We would bring these back to class and read them aloud, whereupon our teacher would confirm the pronunciations and discuss the text's meaning with us.

In the explicitly Christian class taught by Teacher B, we were given one handwritten hymn but otherwise used the New Testament or hymnal exclusively as sources of texts. We did not go through the multistep process of decoding that characterized Teacher E's class. Probably this was because Teacher B's class was primarily for fluent speakers who were learning to perform the reading of syllabary in a very specific Christian environment.

Just as the areas of lexical association with the syllabary in adult and children's language education overlapped but were not exactly coextensive, so the designlike features of the syllabary as presented in children's education spilled over partially into the adult classes. The extent to which the syllabary was treated as designlike in these adult classes varied. Teachers A and C, when presenting the syllabary to students, made their characters deliberately and with all flourishes. Teacher C said that she simplified her writing style when writing fast, but her plan to create a coloring book suggested an attribution of inherent artistic qualities to the syllabary. Outside of class, Teacher A used the syllabary to design beautiful, artistic calendars, which she distributed to one group of students as a reward.

Teacher B pointed out in his class that the "curlicues" generally do not need to be reproduced in handwriting but rather are features of print. Teacher B, however, probably saw writing mainly as an instrument of learning, to be replaced by reading. One's handwriting style was therefore unimportant. Teacher E never modeled or discussed handwriting in his class; his chief interest was the careful decoding of printed text.

An interesting trend emerges out of these (admittedly limited) classroom data on Cherokee language teachers. In the classroom context, men were the exclusive users of easy phonetics, in classes for children as well as for adults. Conversely, all of the women language teachers, including one who did not speak Cherokee fluently, were familiar with and used the syllabary in teaching. Women were also the primary users of syllabary as design. Men played more strongly the role of readers, decoders. This may be why they were the sole users of easy phonetics — easy phonetics represented the ultimate breaking down of the code. It seems possible, therefore, that the design potential of the syllabary (one of its attributed characteristics that makes it suitable for encoding) was largely irrelevant to the men. I will return to this discussion of types of readers and writers in the next chapter.

No matter how the syllabary was used in these classes, it was always used in the presence of the chart. Except in Teacher B's class, where a syllabary-only chart was used, the chart was always the standard one, in which the syllabary characters are arranged alphabetically (for speakers of English), and which offers the standard phonetic equivalents of characters. This chart is always reproduced faithfully, right down to a "standard error" that exists on all copies of the chart that I have ever seen, which is then always "corrected" by users. The two characters ⟨R⟩ and ⟨R⟩, /e/ and /sv/, appear on the chart in such a way that the difference between them is very difficult to reproduce in writing. This is always corrected in handwriting so that one, the /sv/, is much more open than the other, the /e/. Another trick to reading Worcester's standard syllabary chart involves the notes at the bottom. One line reads, "A [is] sometimes sounded *to*" (Holmes and Smith 1977: 2). Presumably, ⟨A⟩ appears in that sentence accidentally, as Scancarelli

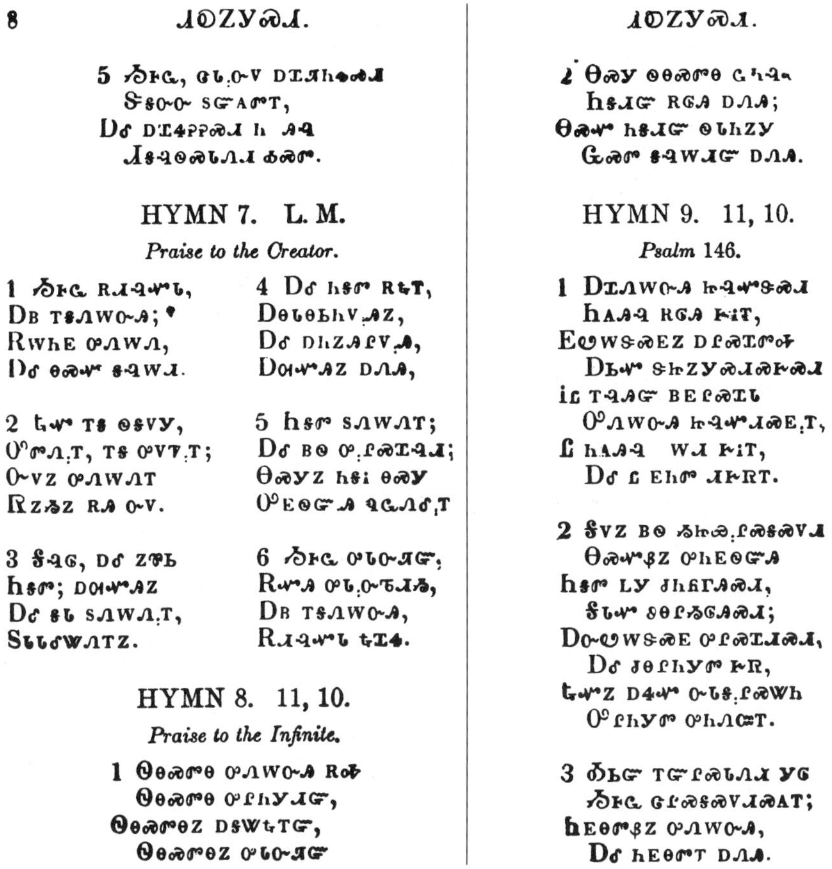

8 ᎠᎤᏅᏏ.

5 ᏏᎦᏓ, ᎬᏓᎣᏫ ᎠᏣᎯᎿᎠᎵ
ᏍᏐᎤᎤ ᏍᎦᎠᏠᎢ,
ᎠᎦ ᎠᎢᎦᏢᏅᎵ Ꮒ ᎠᏇ
ᎠᏍᏏᎣᏅᏗᎵᎵ ᏍᏐᎢᎠ.

HYMN 7. L. M.
Praise to the Creator.

1 ᏏᎦᎬ ᎡᏧᎠᏮᎯ,
ᎠᏴ ᏔᎵᏁᎳᎣᎥ; Ꭷ
ᎡᏫᏂᎡ ᎣᎵᎳᏁ,
ᎠᎦ ᎧᏯᏮ ᏍᎠᏫᎵ.

4 ᎠᎦ ᏂᏍᎢ ᎡᎡᏛ,
ᎠᏗᏆᏂᎥᎾᏃᏂ,
ᎠᎦ ᎠᎲᏃᎠᏞᎥᎠ,
ᎠᎣᎠᏮᎾᏃ ᎠᎵᎠ,

2 ᎬᏮ ᏔᏍ ᏃᎥᎩ,
ᎣᎣᎠᏥ.Ꭲ, ᏔᏍ ᎣᎥᎢᎢ;
ᎣᎥᏃ ᎣᎵᎳᏁᎢ
ᏓᏃᏃ ᎡᎠ ᎣᏫ.

5 ᏂᏍᎢ ᏍᎠᏫᎵᎢ;
ᎠᎦ ᎠᎣ ᎣᏒᎡᎢᎠᏂ;
ᎤᏅᏃ ᏂᏏᎢ ᎤᏅᏯ
ᎣᎣᎡᎣᎬᏗ ᎠᎬᎵᏍᎢ

3 ᏍᎠᎬ, ᎠᎦ ᏃᏒ
ᏂᏍᎢ; ᎠᎣᎠᏮᎾᏃ
ᎠᎦ ᏍᎢ ᏍᎠᏫᎵᎢ,
ᏍᎤᎤᏍᏫᎵᏔᏃ.

6 ᏏᎦᎬ ᎣᎤᎣᎠᎢᎬ,
ᎡᏮᎾ ᎣᎢᎣᎤᏞᏍᎬ,
ᎠᏴ ᏔᏍᎵᎣᎠ,
ᎡᏧᎠᏮᎯ ᎬᎢᏅ.

HYMN 8. 11, 10.
Praise to the Infinite.

1 ᎤᎣᏅᎣᎣ ᎣᎵᎳᎣᎠ ᎡᏆ
ᎤᎣᏅᎣᎣ ᎣᎢᎲᏯᎵᎬ,
ᎤᎣᏅᎣᎣᏃ ᎠᏍᎳᎤᎢᎬ,
ᎤᎣᏅᎣᎣᏃ ᎣᎤᎣᎠᎬ

---

9 ᎠᎤᏅᏏ.

7 ᎤᏅᏯ ᎣᎣᏅᎣᎣ ᎬᏄᎤᎵ
ᏂᏍᎵᎬ ᎡᎬᎠ ᎠᎵᎠ;
ᎤᏅᏮ ᏂᏍᎵᎬ ᎣᏳᎲᏃ
ᎬᏅᎠᎠ ᏍᎠᏫᎵᎬ ᎠᎵᎠ.

HYMN 9. 11, 10.
Psalm 146.

1 ᎠᎢᎳᎣᎤᎠ ᏂᏆᏮᏍᏅᎵ
ᏂᎠᎠᎬ ᎡᎬᎠ ᏂᎢᏔ,
ᎡᏉᏫᏍᏅᎡᏃ ᎠᎵᏅᎢᎣᎥ
ᎠᏴᏮ ᏍᏂᏃᏯᏅᎵᎯᏅᎵ
ᎢᎦ ᏔᏅᎬ ᎡᎡᎵᏅᎢᎤ
ᎣᎣᎵᎳᎣᎠ ᏂᏆᏮᎵᏅᎡ.Ꭲ,
Ꮅ ᏂᎠᎠᎬ ᏭᎵ ᏂᎢᏔ,
ᎠᎦ Ꮅ ᎡᏂᏍ ᎵᏂᎡᏔ.

2 ᏍᎥᏃ ᎠᎣ ᏏᏂᏅᏗᏅᏅᎳ
ᎤᎣᏮᎦᏃ ᎣᏂᎡᎣᎬᎠ
ᏂᏍᎢ ᎺᎩ ᏣᏂᎦᎳᏅᎵ,
ᏍᎬᏮ ᏍᏎᎵᏍᎬᎠᏅᎵ;
ᎠᎣᎡᏉᏫᏍᏅᎡ ᎣᎵᏅᎢᎵᏅᎵ,
ᎠᎦ ᏎᏯᎵᏂᏳᎬ ᎢᎡᏒ,
ᎬᏮᏃ ᎠᏐᎠᏮ ᎣᎤᏍ.ᎵᏅᏪᏂ
ᎣᎣ ᎵᏂᏳᎬ ᎣᏂᎳᎢᏍᎢ.

3 ᏏᏔᎬ ᏔᎬᎵᏅᎵᎵ ᏳᎬ
ᏏᎦᎬ ᎬᎵᏅᏍᏅᎳᏅᏗᎢ;
ᏂᎡᎣᎢᏅᏃ ᎣᎵᎳᎣᎠ,
ᎠᎦ ᏂᎡᎣᎢᏔ ᎠᎵᎠ.

Figure 7. Pages from *Cherokee Hymn Book: Compiled from Several Authors, and Revised* (Asheville, N.C.: Global Bible Society, n.d.).

(1992) has noted; ⟨V⟩ is probably the intended character. But the error is not entirely arbitrary; ⟨V⟩ sometimes appeared as ⟨Λ⟩ in early texts, and the latter is known to have been used by at least one North Carolina syllabary writer to indicate /tho/, as opposed to /to/ (a distinction based on aspiration that the syllabary is incapable of representing).

Yet another trick to reading the syllabary emerges in the context of hymn singing, an activity used by Teacher B and another local Cherokee language Sunday school teacher, as well as in the language preservation project, to teach syllabary (see Figure 7 for a sample page of the hymnal). The Cherokee versions of the hymns were written to match preexisting hymn tunes, and they are generally sung one syllable per note. Occasionally, there is a slight mismatch between the tune and the words so that there is one extra syllable beyond where the sung line ends. These syllables are separated from the rest of the line with a dot, but they are preserved on the printed page. This way, the meaning of the line can be understood, even though it is not sung to its conclusion. A fluent Snowbird resident and social service worker who has sung these hymns for much of her life told me that it was in Teacher B's syllabary class that she first learned the meaning of the "dots," and the reason why the last word is sometimes abbreviated. Once she realized how it worked, she approved of leaving off the last syllable in some cases, "'cause we do that anyway when we speak."

Although the syllabary appeared as codelike to a greater or lesser extent in these classes, the key to the code always had to be present, and there were tricks—in the form of in-group cultural knowledge— even to interpreting the key itself.

Chapter Three

Talking Leaves, Silent Leaves

Syllabary as Code

M

any of the beliefs with which the reader has already become familiar—that the syllabary is an important representation of Cherokee culture and identity, that it is inaccessible or nonphonetic, that it is design-appropriate, that its source is in a universal (and ubiquitous) key, and that it must be faithfully copied—will appear here in new contexts. The foregrounding of the syllabary's iconic and indexical capacities in education that I have summarized by saying that it is treated as a code lays the groundwork for its codelike treatment in the local culture generally.

The hierarchy of writing systems discussed at length in the previous chapter on Cherokee language education reappears here in extremely complex ways. Easy phonetics appeared in a limited number of public spaces in Cherokee while I was there. The only public sign in downtown Cherokee to make use of easy phonetics was a sign with movable lettering in front of one of the churches in the Soco community.[1] This sign sometimes bore the first few lines of the Cherokee version of "Amazing Grace," spelled out in easy phonetics as "Oo-ne-la-nuh-he oo-we-ji i-ga-goo-yuh-he-i / Na-kwo-jo-suh-we oo-lo-se i-ga-goo-yuh-ho-nuh," 'The son of God paid for us / Now he has gone to heaven, he paid for us.' These lines were also frequently reproduced in the weekly bulletin produced by the church. These spellings, although they largely follow the easy principles, have also been influenced by the standard phonetics. The syllable /he/ in the word i-ga-goo-yuh-he-i, for instance, is spelled in the standard fashion. Many of the names listed on the Veterans' Memorial in downtown Cherokee are also written in easy phonetics. The other major source of easy phonetics in the public arena was a book sold to tourists in the downtown shops called *How to Talk Trash in Cherokee* (Grooms and Oocumma 1989). I was surprised when a social services worker from Snowbird told me that the book is greatly enjoyed by some Cherokee readers. What is striking about this book is that it contains material otherwise absent from the self-representations of Cherokee tourism. It addresses topics such as meeting women, drinking, and "talking trash," as the title suggests. It is not coincidental that this book is written in what the authors see as the most basic, easy-to-read, easy phonetics—which are also, of course, the most Anglicized. For example, /siyo/, 'hello,' is written ⟨shee-oh⟩. It is impossible to imagine this book being written in syllabary, both because of the intended reader and because of what is seen as the crudeness of the material. The special code of syllabary would not be appropriate here.

Standard phonetics appeared in many of the commodities produced for sale to tourists, particularly syllabary charts, texts of prayers and hymns reproduced on large pieces of mock parchment, and language educational materials for sale in the shops. International phonetics appeared exclusively in more scholarly language educational materials available in selected shops. The syllabary itself inhabited a patterned distribution throughout the Cherokee landscape, as discussed in other chapters.

The hierarchy among these writing systems was more complex in the world outside the classroom because of the dimensions of commodification and accessibility that shape the syllabary's distribution and functions there. But it was clear that the syllabary continued to be considered an elite mode of writing, not suitable for talking trash or other mundane communications, that it was still treated as the least accessible, most nonphonetic system of those available, and that it was treated as an important icon of Cherokee culture and history and an index of Cherokee cultural identity.

The Iconicity of the Syllabary

Some of the people I spoke with learned to read and write as adults so as to participate in language education or just, as one consultant told me about her literate sisters, to "say they can do it." Many expressed the fear that if they did not learn the syllabary, it would be lost. Some said that Cherokee language, in its written and spoken form, is the crucial element of Cherokee culture and that they wanted to help ensure that it continued.

It was important to many people I interviewed that the syllabary be used and that it be used visibly. But in the most public modes of usage, the syllabary's symbolic capacity to represent meaningful Cherokee utterances directly was downplayed.

Computer fonts have been developed for Cherokee, and one of these was used in the *One Feather* periodically in the mid-1990s to present vocabulary words and short letters. A striking characteristic of this font is that one does not actually have to know the syllabary to use it. It works by taking phonetic spellings and translating them automatically into the appropriate syllabary characters. So although the program produces readable text in the syllabary and makes the syllabary visible to the paper's readership (virtually the entire community), it does not actually require writing in the syllabary. Use of the font thus reinforced the user's sense of the syllabary as a nonphonetic or not centrally phonetic system.

In February 1995, the *One Feather* featured an article titled "Stories from Cherokee Elementary Language Class." These stories, attributed to children in the elementary school, were mostly in English, but they featured Cherokee vocabulary at predictable points, particularly to denote animals. Significantly, the animals were named first in standard phonetics and then in syllabary. The first few sentences read: "One day the yo-na ᎬᎿ was walking and he saw a tsi-sde-tsi ᎶᎤᏚᎵᎢ. The tsi-sde-tsi ᎶᎤᏚᎵᎢ said, 'si-yo' ᏓᎯ, 'I live in Tsa-la-gi ᏣᏴᏱ, do you?' "[2] (*Cherokee One Feather*, 1 February 1995). The article included three stories from elementary school children, all sprinkled with syllabary. The syllabary in these stories was handwritten; it did not make use of the computer font. But just as the font does not require the producer of text to be fully literate in syllabary, so too these texts did not require the reader to be fully literate in it. The phonetic spellings were provided first, assigning the words written in syllabary to a place of secondary communicative significance and a place where they might, in a children's book, be replaced by pictures. This text thus reinforced the perception of the syllabary as both nonphonetic and design-appropriate.

Why work so hard to maintain the visibility of the syllabary at all, one might ask, if it is not central to language learning and if users rely on phonetic spellings anyway? Of course, the answer lies in the syllabary's other semiotic functions, which link it with Cherokee culture and identity. The syllabary thus appeared in all contexts where nonlinguistic elements of Cherokee culture were taught or displayed. Good examples came from the 1993 and 1994 Fall Festivals.

Looking Like Cherokee beyond the Classroom

The Fall Festival is an annual homecoming aimed at both tourists and Cherokees. As well as rides, games, gospel singing, and talent contests, the festival features a large indoor display of local crafts and agricultural products. Adorning the walls in the community room where this display is held are mask designs representing the seven Cherokee clans, with their names in syllabary. Prizes are awarded for the best products on display in various categories. Significantly, the first place prize in needlepoint in 1993 was given to a syllabary chart with Sequoyah at the top.

At the festival, each Cherokee community prepares a display of objects that represents its activities and accomplishments for the year. These displays include home-canned and other agricultural products, crafts and clothing, and perhaps a few newspaper clippings about people in that community. The display from the Yellowhill community, the actual town of Cherokee, contained a child's "alphabet" blocks marked in syllabary. The middle set spelled out ⟨GWY⟩ but the others seemed random, some even upside down, in symmetrical groupings on either side. The same display included a paperback Cherokee New Testament containing a bookmark adorned by the syllabary chart.

The entire back cover of the program to the 1993 Fall Festival was filled by a syllabary chart. An advertisement in the program paid for by the local senior citizens' center, Tsali Manor, reproduced the center's slogan in syllabary: "ᏒᎾ ᏆhᏞᎣᎤᎶᏞ DhᏴᎪ ᏝᎤᎧᎣᏅᎧᎠᎬᎢ," 'where special people meet.'

At the same festival, the Cherokee High School class of 1985 was selling syllabary-adorned T-shirts that read: "ᏣᏩᎩ ᎥᎥᎠᎾᏦᎤᎪ," 'Cherokee Schools,' with "Cherokee + + + Tsalagi" written underneath. They were also offering visitors their names written in syllabary on a small piece of wood.

By being arranged in this setting alongside traditional crafts, foods, and pictures of clan symbols, the syllabary characters were compared with other means of self-representation and accomplishment. At the same time, they were being compared with other objects whose relationship to spoken language is tenuous, if it exists at all.

In 1994, among the crafts on display were glazed black mugs, with the syllabary in the original Sequoyan order in white, and a white and cream glazed teapot, with the syllabary presented in the same order but with slightly more elaborate lettering.[3] A local sporting goods store was selling sweatshirts bearing "ᏣᏩᎩ" and reading "Cherokee Pride" beneath. The "C" in "Cherokee" was decorated with an eagle feather design. At the elders' table, demonstrating beadwork, sat an elderly Cherokee woman wearing one of these sweatshirts. The display of locally grown beans included Cherokee baskets containing several varieties artfully arranged. The winner of this display competition was the largest, but it also featured "ᏣᏩᎩ" spelled out in beans at the center of its design. As in the needlepoint competition from the previous year, the incorporation of syllabary seems to contribute to the positive evaluation of craftwork. Indexically, it identifies the craftsperson as traditional or community-oriented, and at the iconic level, it makes the product "look Cherokee."

Of the 1994 community displays, two included syllabary writing or printing. The Wolftown community display featured a syllabary New Testament, open to John 1:7, propped up among samples of the community's agricultural produce and a piece of bean bread wrapped in hickory leaves. Above the New Testament to the right hung a mandala containing a buffalo skull.

The 1994 community display that most heavily featured syllabic writing, the Snowbird display, won the prize for best community display. Everything in this community's display was labeled in syllabary with the name of its source. The name in syllabary was large and bold, followed underneath in smaller lettering by the person's name in English and the type of craft. So, for example, one label read

> ᏦᏆ ᏯᏗ [artist's pseudonym]
> Quilt Tops

In the middle of the display was a large syllabary chart bearing the heading "ᎬᏘᎩ ᎫᏍᎬᏍᎰᏴᏗ," *tsalaki titehlkwastohti,* 'Cherokee—for learning.' This chart contained no phonetics. Among the dresses, corn, blankets, beans, topographical map of Snowbird, squash, and sauerkraut was displayed a soft-cover syllabary New Testament. A Cherokee woman passing by this display reaffirmed my sense of the value placed on the presence of syllabary when she noted that the Snowbird community deserved to win the award for best display. The main reason, she said, was their prominent use of syllabary.

Syllabary as Design

In the classrooms I visited, the syllabary was held to possess artistic properties that make it suitable as a design in a way that English writing, or phonetic writing of Cherokee, is not. In many other arenas of public life, too, the characters are employed largely for their physical appearance and their general associations.

According to most sources, however, including local consultants, most of the characters do have their origin in written or printed English-language texts. The exact stories of how Sequoyah happened upon this English-language writing vary—some pages floated downstream to him, or he found a diary in the pocket of a dead American soldier during the Creek War—but nevertheless these characters are locally acknowledged to be, at some level, "English" in origin. Just as Cherokee easy phonetics rest on a foundation of presupposed English-language literacy, then, the syllabary itself is acknowledged to have sprung from the inescapable enclosure of the historic Cherokee nation by the larger white American one. But like the normalcy of English-language literacy that is affirmed by the usage of Cherokee easy phonetics, the ubiquity of English lettering is so taken for granted in the local understanding of the syllabary that it disappears as an acknowledged aspect of Cherokee writing, and one hears about it only when specifically asking where Sequoyah got the letters from.[4] Otherwise, their resemblance to English-language letters is nearly completely absent from public discourse. The syllabary's greater suitability as a source of design than English or Cherokee writing, therefore, goes largely unquestioned.

The syllabary chart itself has become a type of design that, in one iconic capsule, refers to the history of Cherokee writing, Cherokee civilization, and Cherokee cultural identity. The chart appears on a number of home and office walls as well as on the keepsakes sold to tourists. But in other cases, the characters are liberated from the chart. For example, the characters have become a very popular form of design for manufactured, stamped Frankoma pottery from Oklahoma, and for North Carolina handmade Cherokee pottery. Most people I talked to agreed that this latter trend was started not long ago by a particular woman potter, a former kindergarten teacher. Significantly, this woman neither read nor "wrote" in the sense of conveying meanings with writing, but she could reproduce the syllabary on paper or clay by heart. If she had privacy, she said, she could write it out in order. She had memorized this order from beginning to end, and if interrupted, she had to go back to the beginning. She thought of the shapes as she produced them, not the associated sounds, which she had not memorized. She could not produce any words in syllabary except ⟨GWY⟩ and her own name. Still, she said, the syllabary was "embedded in her mind like on [her] pottery."

When I first asked the potter about her syllabary pottery, she told me that she got the idea by thinking about the stories her mother told her when she was a child. When these stories came back to her, she wondered why they had such staying power. She said that she had heard of ancient burial urns and seen pottery with intact designs, some a thousand years old. The existence of this ancient pottery she took as evidence that pottery—and the designs it bears—lasts. The syllabary, like these ancient designs, will be "embedded in the clay" of her pottery, preserved like her mother's stories were in her memory. Her hope was that in the future people would know that the Cherokee people had a written language, just as we now have access to knowledge about ancient peoples from their pottery. This woman was clearly motivated by the need for linguistic and cultural preservation, but she implied that her preserved writing would be mute in the future. She did not suggest that in the future people would be able to *read* her pottery; the script on the pottery is not meaningful in that sense. But the existence of the characters on her pottery will point toward a history of meaningful writing, the idea of which was what she was trying to preserve. A Cherokee language teacher echoed this link between the syllabary and cultural preservation when I asked him if he thought the existence of the syllabary would support the preservation of the Cherokee language. He answered, "Yeah . . . because after you're dead, there won't be anybody to hear you speak, so your writing will be here."

The pottery became so popular that several members of this potter's family started to make it, although she reported that they did not always reproduce the characters faithfully and in the proper order. Even though the characters were functioning as design elements in this context, there was a right and wrong way to produce them to preserve the heritage of Cherokee writing accurately. If the order was not accurate, she said, the pottery could create confusion among those actually attempting to write or just to piece the system together. Indeed, when she decorated smaller pieces, like mugs, with syllabary, she usually could not fit the entire set of characters on one piece. To preserve the integrity of the system, however, she picked up on the next piece, at the top and circling down, where she left off on the first one. This way, she said, if the pottery is discovered in the future, those who happen upon it will eventually discover the whole system. It was equally important that the characters be readable—she had seen the stamped Oklahoma syllabary pottery and found it unacceptable because the characters are "matted together," not "readable like we do it."

At the same time that she emphasized the importance of preserving the system and the evidence that the Cherokees had functioning writing, she explicitly compared the syllabary to the other designs she used on pots, noting that her other designs, too, created with brushes and peach pits, will be preserved. She told me that among her other rationales for decorating her pottery with syllabary was the fact that it "makes a good design," particularly because she used Sequoyah's original characters, complete with the "tails and swirls in Sequoyah's handwriting."[5]

Probably the most striking example of the syllabary characters functioning as chart-free design was the marquee of the Sequoyah Cafeteria (Figure 3), a downtown business that has since closed. Until the business changed hands in the mid-1990s, this sign with its colorful neon border composed of syllabary characters occupied a prominent place right in the heart of downtown Cherokee. Despite the presence of a portrait of Sequoyah himself at the top of the sign, the tourist driving by would already have to be somewhat familiar with the syllabary to recognize the characters as such rather than as a flashy, though somewhat irregular, designed border. Not only did the syllabary portion of the sign come across as meaningless, but it seemed so *obviously* meaningless that, according to the owner, no visitor or local person had ever *asked* if it had a meaning.

Syllabary clocks, and watches even more so, have become popular in Cherokee. These clocks and watches are of note because there are no numeric symbols in Sequoyah's system (he developed a set of numerals, but they were never adopted); each number is represented by the Cherokee *word* for that number (see Figure 4). Many Cherokees do not in fact read the syllabary, and therefore probably do not read the words for these numbers, except perhaps as sight-words, but in the context of a clock face, reading ability becomes irrelevant. The clock face provides the context necessary for comprehension. These Cherokee words, like any other objects, can represent units of time because of how they are placed.

The role of the syllabary in hymn singing to some degree parallels its role in these timepieces. In both cases, the characters' positioning within an established structure, independently of users' syllabary literacy, imbues the characters with function and meaning. The hymns can be sung properly by those not fluent in Cherokee, because the song structure removes the pressure to produce accurate intonation and vowel length. The song's rhythm also makes it easier to locate consonant clusters, which the syllabary generally does not represent. But most important, for many hymn singers the words to the hymns have been familiar all their lives. Thus, although the hymnal is usually held and looked at, the songs do not really have to be read at all by most singers. Although the characters could not be said to be functioning as a design in this context, the situation is similar in that their appearance in culturally specific forms and contexts is often what matters most.

When the characters were used as designs, then, their ability to represent sound and convey specific meaning was pushed aside. Their ability to do so was not irrelevant; the characters are eye-catching and even exotic to outsiders, partly because of their history as the writing of a "civilized tribe," vaguely understood though that history may be by tourists. Whole words may even function as designs—in pendants that bear ⟨GWY⟩, in the clan names arranged in a circular pattern, on the walls of the elementary school. My point is not that no one is capable of reading the words in these contexts, but that the words occur in contexts where designs would otherwise occur, on ceramics, jewelry, colorful elementary school boards that contain pictures, and where knowing their specific (symbolic) meaning is not essential.

Decoding the Syllabary

We have seen that many of the characteristics attributed to the syllabary in the classroom, and that contribute to its overall codelike status—its high visibility yet low inherent communicative functionality, its importance as a design, its service as an icon for Cherokee culture—are reproduced in the community at large. So, too, the chart, the key to the code, is just as omnipresent in adult social contexts as it is in the schools. Many homes and offices contain the chart. Adult Cherokees, many of whom see the syllabary as difficult or inaccessible, rarely try to learn it without the use of this ubiquitous, Rosetta stone-like key. The functioning of the chart as a key is underscored by the fact that most Cherokees use the chart to move from the syllabary to the standard phonetics in a unidirectional fashion. That is, readers generally use the chart to decode syllabary writing into phonetic writing, just in reading to themselves, or in writing out a hymn or Bible passage for themselves or others.

The codelike treatment of the syllabary came together with a certain coherence around the theme of revelation. The syllabary was seen as difficult in a way that set it apart from the phonetic systems. Whereas with phonetic writing, the struggle is in the process of agreeing upon the values of letters and upon the appropriate breadth or narrowness of transcription, usage of the syllabary seemed to involve more specifically questions of knowledge. Asking if someone "knows" the syllabary implies (and is possibly coterminous with) a host of other questions: Does he or she know the values of the characters? Does he or she know the language? Does he or she know the culture? Does he or she know the Bible? Unlike phonetics, syllabic writing is a window onto knowledge, and it has the capacity to open and shut.

Adult Cherokees literate in the syllabary told me that some days they were able to read it fine, and then the next day their ability seemed to disappear. One Cherokee language teacher told me that, in contrast to English, he finds it easy to read Cherokee some days and hard others. He felt this might be because of the absence of "intonational markers" in the syllabary, but "there [was] something mysterious about it as well." He teaches a Cherokee language Sunday school class for adults, and told me that other members of the class had the same on-again, off-again relationship with syllabary reading. I was able to confirm this when I visited the class. The characters were seen as elusive. When another Sunday school teacher worked at the church, my consultant told me, he would copy words in syllabary over into extremely large handwriting, so as to "grasp them better."

Another consultant implied that learning the syllabary was more than just memorizing the phonetic values of its characters. Some of them, she told me, "I don't understand." Her use of the word "understand," rather than, for example, "know," suggested that there is meaning beyond the purely phonetic value, which must be grasped in learning the syllabary.

Some users saw the ability to read and write Cherokee—particularly to read it—as a channel of direct access to information, or even salvation. One Snowbird woman told me that reading the Bible in the syllabary "makes it all clear." Although Cherokee was her first language, she is fully bilingual, so the issue is not her English-language competency. She has heard preachers reading from the Cherokee New Testament all her life, but being able to do so herself is somehow better. It gives her a deeper understanding. For her, Cherokee is more than a first language—it is her God-given language, the appropriate language in which to hear and read the word of God.

Like many in her community, this woman has learned to read and write Cherokee as an adult. She said that she sometimes got out of practice because of the limited opportunities to read and write Cherokee. Reading the Bible in the syllabary is therefore more difficult and time-consuming, she says, than reading in English. But the results are more complete, the understanding more satisfying. To her, there is a sense of perfect transparency to the syllabary when it is used in this context.

Another Snowbird resident told me, "When you [are] reading Cherokee Indian Bible, it *tells you as you read it.* And when you read the English Bible, then you have to go look up somewhere else, as a reference . . . the Cherokee Bible, as you read it, it *explains to you what's what*" (emphasis added).

This attribution of utter clarity to the syllabary in the context of Bible reading might seem puzzling in light of the fact that many local preachers, including some Cherokee ones, urge their congregations to abandon many aspects of traditional Cherokee culture. In one church I visited, I heard an Oklahoma Cherokee lecture the North Carolina Cherokee congregation, "It's fine to remember where we come from, but more important to know where we're going." In other words, he continued, "Don't let tradition send you to Hell." But clearly this anti-tradition message does not apply to the Cherokee language, and particularly to the production and use of printed syllabary, for the preservation of which, in North Carolina at least, the churches have been largely responsible. In this context, the Cherokee language and the written documents produced in it are supercultural—so transparent that their cultural specificity is superseded. When I asked adult language Teacher B why he had reprinted an 1880 syllabary pamphlet containing the Baptist Articles of Faith, when so few people would be able to read it, he answered, "because it's the truth!"

While its cultural specificity was overshadowed in this context, the syllabary *was* seen by many literate Cherokees I talked to as a tool given by God to them as a group. They believed, therefore, that they should use and preserve it. Some even expressed the belief that if they did not use it, God would ask them what they have done with it and punish them.

There is a tension in this belief that the syllabary is a God-given source of access to the Truth. The source of that tension lies in the fact that the syllabary, in handwritten rather than printed form, has been equally instrumental in the preservation of non-Christian traditional culture. From the Christian point of view, the syllabary can provide access to the wrong sort of knowledge, as well as to the Truth, and some of the adults I interviewed were quick to distinguish the type of reading and writing they do from that done by traditional Cherokee medicine men.

The Code's Relationship to Sacred Text

Most adults whom I saw write in the syllabary modeled their writing after print, as the school teachers do, and wrote deliberately, almost scribally, including all flourishes. Most copied hymns or Bible verses and did not do much creative writing in the syllabary. Attempting to emulate printing is laborious and inefficient; the fact that most literate Cherokees nevertheless write this way may be a measure of how little writing they actually do, but it also indexes the importance of having printlike handwriting.

The traditional writing of medicinal texts (sometimes called formulas) by medicine men may have been only slightly less constrained. Although these texts were generally intended as very precise records of received oral formulas, and thus were not spontaneously generated by individuals, each contained information that was potentially the unique property of the individual. Therefore, it was held to be very important that others did not fully crack the user's particular syllabary code. Handwriting in such texts, therefore, was not iconically modeled after print, but was as unique and unreadable as the author could make it. Such syllabary handwriting, then, differently from the copying of print, doubly encoded a particular text: not just syllabary, it was also the handwriting of a particular individual. The possession of such handwriting also indexically marked the possessor as a member of a special group—as a medicine man—and further marked him as a reading group of one. Ideally, only he could fully decode his own texts.

These medicinal texts were rarely discussed with outsiders in the 1990s. Some people felt that the possession and use of these notebooks conflicted with their Christianity. Still, several people I talked to said their families still possessed such books. There seemed to be considerable demand for the knowledge these notebooks contained and at the same time an ambivalence toward them on the part of their owners.

Some people distinguished between formulas for medicine or curing and those for magic or conjuring. Conjuring in particular was seen by some as being in tension with or incompatible with Christianity.

A resident of the Snowbird community told me that his handwriting is modeled after print, like that found in the Bible, whereas the handwriting in a conjurer's notebook is altered and simplified (he did not distinguish conjuring from medicine). As a Christian, he said, he has no business writing like that. His printlike handwriting is intended to index his Christianity. He told me, "I've seen a few of the, you know, what the old medicine men used, and, what you call that, witchcraft, stuff like that? But I don't do that none. . . . The Lord helped me to learn my Cherokee. And I don't want to fool with none of that stuff, you know, it's not no good."

He went on to tell me that he modeled his handwriting after the standard chart, and contrasted this with the writing of medicine men. "That old like medicine man stuff," he said, "they don't write it like that. It's different like . . . they don't have most of . . . the markings, the little extra marks on 'em." "Plainer?" I asked. "Yeah. Well, they're kinda more like towards just the regular English letters. . . . You know, like some of them, like that, like that 't,' you know, they'd just be just like a 't,' straight." Handwriting that is simple, unlike print, and, at least in this case, that approaches English-language lettering in appearance, indexes a straying from Christianity.

A Yellowhill resident described the handwriting of her father, a medicine man, in the following way: "Daddy, he had different ways of writing his syllables. There was one syllable that he would write like two 5's together, and I never knew. That's why I couldn't read his writing. It was better for him to write it that way than the way it was on the syllabary [chart]." She went on to explain that the characters on the syllabary chart are difficult to "copy." For the medicine man, then, the advantage of using idiosyncratic handwriting is dual: it is easier to write than if one copied the New Testament–style printing, and it also obscures his texts from would-be copiers.

One Cherokee language teacher was quite confident that his aunt's syllabary handwriting never looked like anything other than the print in the New Testament, even though he may have been quite young when observing it. Since he was not yet literate in syllabary at the time he observed his aunt writing, it seems remarkable that he knew what form her writing took. Nevertheless, the iconic similarity between his aunt's handwriting and biblical print was clearly important to him. When I asked whether he noticed any difference between her handwriting and the printed syllabary found in the New Testament, he said, "No, it was the same, come to think of it, it was the same. It was all the same. . . . The house that she lived in burned down not too long ago, . . . and there were a few words . . . in that house yet that she . . . wrote, and they were the same." I mentioned that I understood that in the past there was greater variation in syllabary handwriting than there is today, to which he replied, "Yeah, but they were the same, 'cause I remember. I can remember."

The combination of the utter transparency of printed syllabary as a window onto God's word and its role as an index of Christian faith may explain why this teacher and one of his relatives told me in another conversation that it was wrong to alter the wording of the New Testament to reflect local dialect. You have to "read it just the way it is," they told me. When I suggested that some readers might substitute the syllable /tsa/ for the syllable /tla/ (which does not occur in most North Carolina dialects), they objected: "You can't do that. God don't change." The transparency of printed syllabary, their comments suggest, goes hand in hand with its immutability.

The syllabary print, as found in the New Testament, is also considered to be the original and official version of the syllabary, even though it bears little resemblance to the system first perfected by Sequoyah. When I discussed Sequoyah's original order for the syllabary, as well as his scriptlike writing style, with the public school Cherokee language teacher, he said, "I always go by this one, the one in the Testament, written a long time ago, the original. . . . You asked, how do I know which one is right. Since this is down in the Testament, when you check the words, you'll see they're all used, and they all come out right. So I'm convinced these are in the right order. . . . After we read and study all these verses, look back [pointing to the chart in the front of the New Testament], all these fitting just like our alphabet. That's why I'm convinced this is it."

The printed syllabary in the New Testament is self-justifying, then. It is right because it is internally consistent—that is, the appearance and phonemic assignment of the characters in the chart in the front match their appearance and use throughout the Testament. One might suggest that one model for verifying the truth of the Bible itself was being applied by my consultant to the question of the syllabary's authenticity and correctness.

The following story of how a woman's reading skills became the focus of a struggle between her father (a medicine man) and her husband (a would-be conjurer) should illustrate the complexity of the relationship between these various types of reading and writing and the knowledge with which they are associated. Print, syllabary, Christianity, "conjuring," revelation, and obfuscation all come into play in this one episode of text sharing.

About fifteen years before our interview, this woman learned to read under considerable pressure from her husband. She wanted to read her father's notebooks, according to her, strictly for the medicinal information. Unbeknownst to her, her husband was interested in the conjuring formulas that the notebooks also contained. She learned to read, using a process that many Cherokees have told me they use. On her own, she read the Bible and hymn book in Cherokee, referring to the chart in the front of each book for the standard phonetics, writing these under each syllabary character, and then reading these texts until the syllabary itself was sufficiently familiar to her. Having done this, she presented herself to her father, with her studies as a credential that she felt would gain her access to the notebooks. She described her conversation in the following way: "I said, 'bout the Indian book, your medicine book. I said, . . . I've been doing a lot of studying, and I think I can read. I said, . . . I checked myself on the—the Indian testament. He said it's a good thing to do. I said, well, I checked myself on that, and then, . . . a book what Joe brought home [*Poor Sarah*, a Christian narrative], I said I read it through, well, you know, reading in Indian. And I said the Indian hymn book, I can understand what those words are. He said that's good, he said you done good. I said, so now I wanna see if I can read one of your books, [on] medicine. He said, on medicine? I said yeah, I said that's the only thing I wanna learn, is about medicine."

He approved of her self-training, not entirely because she now possessed the technical skill of reading. She also had the moral credential of having learned in the way she did. This was necessary, because her father, who had struggled with the relationship between his knowledge of conjuring and his Christianity, wanted to be sure that she was capable of sorting the notebooks' contents—picking out the medicinal formulas and ignoring the ones that had to do with "conjuring." In fact, he drew up a special table of contents for her, telling her where to find only the medicinal formulas. The skill she had gained by reading the Bible, though helpful, probably would not be sufficient in helping her to read the notebooks anyway, since, as her father told her, handwriting and print in the syllabary can be quite different. In fact, she did find his handwriting quite difficult to read, and she believes he may have cultivated his handwriting with obfuscation in mind, as a way of protecting his knowledge. It was not only the technical training in reading, then, but the assertion of Christian identity that goes hand in hand with reading for most Cherokees, that he wanted her to have before turning over his books.

Her husband, who had neither the ability to read nor the moral credential provided by having gone through this experience of self-teaching, was in fact mainly interested in the magical elements of the books and tried to get my consultant to recite them to him over and over again. In frustration, she finally returned the books to her father.

Certain types of knowledge or enlightenment, then, were seen as accessible only through an ability to read the syllabary, *and* they were seen as potentially hidden by the syllabary. It is significant that my consultant's father did not offer to tell her his formulas orally or to translate them for her. Preachers with Cherokee-speaking congregations, similarly, encouraged their congregations to learn the syllabary so that they might read the Bible for themselves, even though most were quite fluent in English, and though they already had the opportunity to hear the Cherokee translation read by another speaker.

The revelational-obfuscatory nature of the syllabary made its way beyond the church walls as well, and the syllabary's usefulness as a code is even articulated overtly by some. Elementary school language Teacher 1 told me that she used the syllabary "if [she wanted] to write something [but didn't] want the kids to know what it says, 'cause . . . none of them were really that well versed yet." Later, she added that she used the same technique at home "when [she didn't] want [her] husband to know."

An elderly resident of the Snowbird community and former Chero-

kee language teacher moved quickly to a discussion of the code potential of the language itself when I asked about advantages of being literate in syllabary. He told me,

> If I was to call [my niece] in here, and I wanted to talk or some-
> thing, that I didn't want you to know about, well, I could switch
> over to Cherokee language, and I could communicate with her. . . .
> That's one advantage we got. And that's the same way with the
> Cherokee language, you know, back in the war days, I guess you've
> heard about . . . all those people [who] were breaking the code,
> you know, and they knew where all the enemies were. Every time,
> you know, the United States sent a code out there, they broke the
> code, they knew what was going on. Until you know, they got
> two Indian boys that spoke Cherokee. All right, the command-
> ing [officer] told this Indian, said you send this signal off to the
> other, and they had another Indian on the other end. When they
> sent this signal off there, in our language, though, they couldn't
> do nothing with that language—they couldn't break the code on
> that, so uh . . . to me, that's the advantage. So . . . I'm just proud
> to be a Cherokee. Proud to be an Indian.[6]

Types of Readers, Writers, and Knowledge

It should be clear that local presuppositions concerning how the syllabary works or ought to be used differed from one context to the next.
The presupposed relationship between writing on the one hand and
spoken Cherokee, specific referents, and types of knowledge on the
other ranged from very direct (where the syllabary was seen as nearly
transparent) to nearly severed (where the syllabary drew for its "meaning" on the general history of Cherokee writing and the broader cultural context).

In design mode, and when used for cultural self-identification, the
syllabary enjoyed little relationship to spoken Cherokee or to specific
referents. When syllabic printing was being copied, as in, most commonly, the copying of Bible verses, its relationship to a particular religious content was affirmed. At the same time, users were enacting a
hierarchy, in which print is the primary form of syllabic characters,

with handwriting being an imitation thereof. They were also maintaining a link with Samuel Worcester's primal act of "codification"
that prototypically established two elements of contemporary Cherokee writing: the chart as the key to the syllabic code, and the form of
print to be considered standard. Simultaneously, they were drawing on
a shared understanding of that moment in time when the newly codified print was put into use in the first edition of the *Cherokee Phoenix,*
and as work began on the translation of the New Testament—the same
translation, indeed the same exact text, that people use today to learn
to read and write.

These relationships were not only apparent in the structured distribution of syllabary in the visual landscape of the Cherokee community,
but they were also both demonstrated and enacted through various
types of embodied reading and writing practice and forms of material
production. Being a "reader," a "writer," a "copier," a "possessor," a
"teacher"—each of these relationships to the syllabary implied a particular form of practice that indexically constituted each type of user
differently.

These categories of syllabary users mapped onto other categories
of Cherokee social differentiation in interesting ways. For example,
Cherokee men seemed more likely to be accomplished "readers," both
of scripture (this practice tending to produce Sunday school teachers)
and of medicinal/magical texts (this practice tending to produce medicine men/conjurers). "Reading" here refers to a frequently performative act; reading silently to oneself was probably a less significant category of usage than reading aloud. Men were also more often "writers,"
in the specific sense of producing texts that are not copied from other
texts. This category would include a consultant who had just begun
writing songs in the syllabary, a Cherokee man who produces syllabary tombstones, and, traditionally, medicine men. Women were more
likely to be secular teachers of the syllabary, and thus they produced
more blackboard writing and handouts in syllabary. Women were also
much more likely to use the syllabary to create designs. "Hymn singing," a special type of "reading," was one productive activity in which
men and women seemed to participate equally.

It is especially important to note that reading, writing, and copying
were largely divorced as practices. Reading, or "de-coding," the New

Testament was for most readers a performative demonstration of faith. On the other hand, one of the only reasons to "en-code," that is, to create texts with new or inaccessible content, was if one were a medicine man/woman or conjurer. From the Christian point of view, the Truth, and the only content of significance, has already been encoded. Given this, it is understandable that Christians frequently read John 1—"In the beginning was the word and the word was God"—over and over again in their effort to learn the syllabary. The "word," as reflected in the New Testament, and God have the same timeless beginning and immutability.

The New Testament and hymnal could be copied, but their content generally could not be obscured or altered. Medicine men, too, traditionally transcribed formulas in exacting, precise detail without alteration. But frequently such texts were transcripts made from oral versions and they then became private, inheritable property. Whereas the Bible is generally copied so as to increase its circulation and accessibility, a medicine man's formulas were traditionally transcribed so as to limit both.

Therefore, the best possible quality a Christian writing system, and the texts produced in it, can have is utter transparency. Furthermore, it is fitting that this transparency takes work to achieve. One respected elder from Big Cove told me that he disapproves of the simplification of the Bible, revisions that make it easier to read. This is wrong, he said; "the Bible is not supposed to be changed by one letter." You have to work for understanding, for this spiritual food, just as you have to work to put food on the table, he said. The tool with which one accomplishes this work, and one of the most important texts that can be possessed in this mode, is the chart, the key to the code. Without this tool, this key, the message is impossible to read.

Reading and writing syllabary is a specialization by nature. One must feel "called" to do it. Outside of the context of traditional medicine, the callings tend to take one of two forms—one associated with cultural preservation and the other associated with Christian salvation and sobriety. Cultural preservationists often told me that they wanted to teach the language and syllabary to those Cherokees who don't know it out of fear of linguistic and cultural loss. Many Christian Cherokees literate in the syllabary told me that they learned how to read and write as part of the process of entering the church as adults, or as their faith matured, at about thirty years old. When I asked one Snowbird man how he learned the syllabary, he said, "Well, they always tell me, when [you] wanna learn something, ask the Lord to help you. So I prayed about it, you know, and I studied hard, too. And I knowed enough English to read there where it says how the sounds go, like they do in English, with the short 'a,' and long 'a,' and stuff like that. And I just kept studying on it, and every time I'd read one of the alphabets, you know, I'd write it down, and I just kept doing that, and I learned just in about a month's time, I guess. I was able to read pretty good then."

Another consultant told me that she had not learned the syllabary yet because she had not heard the call. I asked her if she had thought about learning, and she said, "Well, I think, one of these days, when I feel led to, you know, [by] God."

Some had experiences as children in which parents or grandparents tried to teach them the syllabary as part of Bible study, or less formally by using the Bible or hymnal. I asked adult language Teacher A when she first encountered the syllabary as meaningful writing. "Maybe eleven, twelve years old, I'm not sure when I first remember seeing the Bible, and then the song book, then hearing the elders sing the Cherokee songs. And then, as I got older, my mother showed me . . . still in my teen years, my mother showed me a word in the Bible, which was all written in Cherokee language, and she showed me a word in there, a two-syllable word, which was the word for Jesus, and that's the only one, evidently, that she could read, too, and you know, she showed me that, and [laughing] that's the one that I could read!" But for most of my consultants, mastery of the entire writing system came later, when the person became a responsible adult member of a particular parish.

Not every member of the community followed this progression, however, and the total number of adults literate in the syllabary remains small. Literacy in the syllabary is a specialization, not a matter of basic adult competency.

As Benedict Anderson (1983) pointed out (with reformulation in Silverstein 1994), in its print form, writing has been seen by many communities of speakers as having the capacity to bring certain dialects closest to a "standard," to "a language of power." That is, speakers frequently grant a privileged position to writing and any dialect it represents, possibly even allowing print to "correct" their own speech. Anderson has also theorized that print allows for the creation of "imagined communities," groups of readers who imagine themselves sharing simultaneous experiences with other, similar readers, thus contributing to the growth of what we now call nationalism. Literacy is thereby the ticket with which one enters such a community or the experience of it.

In Cherokee, where perhaps 5 to 10 percent of the population speaks Cherokee, and fewer are literate in the syllabary, the situation is obviously quite different. If literacy in syllabary does contribute to the coherence of this community, it is not by virtue of the fact that reading is a shared, simultaneous activity, in imagination or otherwise. Nor does this community generally experience the circulation of multiple copies of printed texts in syllabary—texts that, like a newspaper, readers can be expected to consume within a given time period, texts that bring news intended for individual members of the community to read for themselves. Rather, there is a relatively finite set of texts being circulated in printed syllabary—these consisting most centrally of the Cherokee New Testament and hymnal, with occasional additions of new religious texts. Individuals who can read syllabary frequently read as performance—either by reading aloud from the New Testament or by singing a hymn from the hymnal. (The latter is often a special kind of performativity, however, in which the singer knows the words by heart, and therefore may or may not be reading in the typical sense the song text held dutifully in his or her hands.) Readers of the Cherokee New Testament are frequently Sunday school teachers or other prominent congregation members, and their performances are often offered for the benefit of nonreaders. Being able to read syllabary in the context of a local church indexes religious devotion and characterizes the reader as a source of knowledge and wisdom in Christian spiritual matters generally. Those who sing Cherokee hymns (and in appearance, at least, this means they can read Cherokee hymns) are likewise sought after, there being a special demand for them to sing at the bedsides of the sick, the gospel sings that also function as community fund-raisers, and wakes.

Rather than allowing them to enter into a community of readers and writers, then, as in the mainstream American model of literacy acquisition, or as in Anderson's (1983) scenario, literacy in syllabary distinguishes adult Cherokees and gives them highly specialized social roles to play. Mastery of this code indexes membership in a select group, maturity, religious devotion, and cultural expertise.

Both reading and writing, considered as embodied practices, contribute to the constitution of multiple subjects—what might variously be called "readers," "writers," "producers of writing," "circulators of writing," and "consumers of writing"—and to the constitution of a community with a given shape. The actual embodied practice engaged in most frequently by readers of Cherokee print is an oral performance, in the context of an audience composed of kin and fellow parishioners. This reader, not as a communicator of new, individual meanings, but as a vehicle of access to the common word, serves as the locus for the smallest community unit, the church congregation within the Cherokee subcommunity. He or she is a focal point lending coherence to these smaller units around which Cherokee social life revolves. The distribution of syllabary readers, then, iconically represents the structure of Eastern Cherokee religious and social organization. It is the measured *distribution* of readers throughout the larger community that suggests its structure and not the autonomous yet simultaneous actions of community-minded individuals.

Certainly the latter type of experience of a sense of community could be said to exist in Cherokee, but it exists via English-language literacy. When nearly every household and business is tuned in to the Cherokee tribal council meetings each month, held in English, a shared and defining community activity is taking place. But the circulation and consumption of printed syllabary text is an icon of another type of community, one in which a much smaller group is the relevant social unit, and in which group cohesion, deference, and an acknowledgment of the asymmetry of knowledge are more important than shared individual experiences.

The Logic of Training

The way the syllabary was introduced to children in the schools in the mid-1990s was significantly related to the ways in which it has been used in Cherokee society generally. Not just any code, this is a culturally specific Cherokee code, the use of which is privileged and to some extent mysterious. What children were doing in the Cherokee language classroom modeled what the adults in their community were doing and what, presumably, they might later do themselves. If they follow the patterns set by the adults around them, they will use Cherokee in very specific ways, not congruent with their uses of written English.

Although some of the children in Cherokee language education may grow up to become syllabary readers, not all will, if they follow the pattern of their parents and grandparents. In fact, not all should, according to the cultural logic of syllabary literacy distribution. If it were universal, how could literacy serve as a measure of maturity, a certain place in the life trajectory, and unusual Christian devotion? Indeed, local beliefs reflected in my interviews ran counter to the objective of universal literacy, as the following story illustrates.

One of the very few Cherokees under thirty who was literate in the syllabary in the mid-1990s told me how he was first taught to read by his grandfather.

> Yeah, it was, I guess, about when I was age thirteen. I was sitting on the porch with my grandfather, and he was already pretty sick with the chemotherapy that he was taking for [cancer] and he just one day just started talking about the Cherokee alphabet, and how it was used and things. Well, he just took out a carpenter's pencil and then a brown paper bag, a brown shopping bag, started writing down the symbols that he could remember, and their sounds. And . . . I guess he wrote down about twelve of 'em. And he was teaching me at that time how, you know, that you put 'em together, what they say, you know is the basic thing you have to remember. How—what they look like and what they say, so that's the first step. Second step he said is how to conjugate them together to make complete words. And then he said then the third step would be sentence structure. Putting 'em in a structure of sentences. So he went down and just remembered— recalled from memory as to how he remembered the Cherokee symbols as being written. Then eventually he found that alphabet chart that he had. He went down that way. He explained to me that there was six vowels that covered the Cherokee language, as any language in the world, he said. Six vowels. Then he took the

alphabet chart, starting with the six vowels, went down, down the row vertically, and then went horizontally with the consonant sounds, and you know, he conjugated them all together, and I guess we got about to row four on the alphabet when he just couldn't—he couldn't go any further, he couldn't remember. So I, after he died, I was—I had a hard time. I didn't think about it no more. I never thought about what he had told me about the alphabet and stuff, you know, so it just brought back bad memories.

About two years later, however, he went back to the syllabary and completed teaching himself how to read and write. But his efforts were not met with universal approval.

> I was at one time accused—I was accused—I was accused at one time, oh, I just hate to use that word—I guess [of] witchcraft. Being so young, and knowing that . . . Someone had made a statement to one of my relatives that someone's training him, or someone's teaching him, because they said that there's no other reason why a person should know that at a young age. You know, then I thought, well, I better be reserved with this as to how I use it and stuff because people will get that impression, you know. I didn't know what to think about that, but then I kind of threw that feeling off. I thought, at least I know what I'm using it for, you know, let them people formulate their own ideas about it. So you know, I didn't let it bother me anymore, but that had been passed across the table at one time, that someone was training me (laughing) cause it was in my family at one time, the older people in my family, they were known for that. They—I guess they were just under the assumption that that's what it was for. I learned it 'cause I wanted—'cause my grandpa wanted me to. (Laughing)

This community attitude would seem to stand in tension with a language education program that includes the teaching of the syllabary to young children. However, as we have seen, the syllabary has been incorporated into the Cherokee language curriculum in a very careful and specialized way.

If Cherokee language education does continue to expand, the resulting program will not be like other second-language education programs in the tribal schools. After all, Cherokee is *not* a second language in this community, and the ways in which Cherokee is taught and used will not necessarily be patterned after English or any other language. The fact that the syllabary is not functioning as the primary writing system for teaching Cherokee does not represent any fault or lack on the part of teachers or students. Rather, it reflects a respect for the particular nature and appropriate usage of the syllabary. Because the Cherokees had begun producing written documents in English translation before they had the benefit of Sequoyah's system, and because alternative systems for writing Cherokee have been available since Sequoyah's time, it has always been possible to see the syllabary as special and not necessarily appropriate for all types of writing, writers, or readers.

This orientation toward the syllabary as a unique writing system, although it is not overtly communicated, was evident in the behavior of children I observed. In one elementary school class, the children made cards to send to family or friends for a holiday. Almost all students asked the teachers to show them how to write their names in syllabary, so that they could sign their cards this way. Many of the children recognized the appearance of their name in the syllabary, although they didn't know the phonetic spelling or pronunciation. These children may have found it natural to write their names with the syllabary because proper names are more susceptible to the use of codes, like nicknames and signatures, than are other words, and because the meaning and pronunciation of proper names are often learned through interaction rather than reading. The opacity of the syllabary thus may not have been an issue. Using the syllabary makes the cards "look" Cherokee and asserts the identity of their creators *as* Cherokee. This was true whether the students could pronounce the syllabary words or not. The boy who wrote ⟨Ꮗ⟩ three times in the middle of a sea of his own name may also have been engaging in this kind of iconic-indexical communication. Use of the syllabary in such a context may say in a very general sense, "I am Cherokee."

The syllabary was also manipulated by children in order to set boundaries. One day, I was studying in Cherokee's public library for a Cherokee language class I was taking. A Cherokee boy and girl were in the library as well, doing homework. The boy came and sat at my table, while the girl remained at the table nearby. The library was nearly empty, so I wondered at this move. They had noticed, apparently, that I was attempting to read and write in the syllabary. The girl at the nearby table began passing notes in syllabary to her friend at my table. The boy apparently could not read syllabary, for the author had to keep coming to our table to "decode" her messages. In the conventional sense, there was no literate exchange taking place by way of the syllabary between these two children. But their actions were rich in potential meanings—about their pride in their own skills, about the humorousness of my attempts to write, about who should be reading and writing syllabary in the library after school.

Chapter Four

Reading the Signs

*Metalinguistic Characterizations
of the Syllabary*

*T*his chapter takes us from the relatively unconscious, unarticulated cultural presuppositions about the syllabary mobilized in
its iconic and indexical use and summarized in the trope of the
code, to users' conscious and articulated beliefs about the syllabary's
relationship to the spoken Cherokee language. These linguistic ideologies help to justify the syllabary's codelike functioning and help to
explain why the syllabary's potential for representing the sounds of
spoken Cherokee is so problematized.

The most obvious of these articulated beliefs is the notion that
there is something in Cherokee resembling what Bloomfield (1964) described as "literate" speech, and that such speech has as its source the
written, syllabic versions of words. This belief, though it may seem
straightforward, is fraught with contradictions and sociolinguistic implications.

Prior to my arrival in Cherokee, as a nonspeaker learning about the
Cherokee language and syllabary, I had been under somewhat mixed
impressions about the relationship between the syllabary and the spoken language. It certainly seemed miraculous that any one person, particularly one who had no prior knowledge of writing in any language,
could isolate and represent the phonemes of his language in written
symbols. Furthermore, I was struck by how much more efficient, or
transparent, the relationship seemed to be between written Chero-

kee in the syllabary and the sound shape of spoken Cherokee, than is the relationship between written and spoken English. I had also read and heard a good deal about the limits of the syllabary—in particular, its failures to include ways of indicating vowel length, pitch, intrusive h, and glottal stop, as well as its inability to always distinguish voiced from unvoiced and aspirated from unaspirated consonants. Once I began putting the syllabary to use, I noticed that because every syllabary character, with the exception of ⟨Ꮝ⟩, /s/, indicates the presence of a vowel, syllabic writing tends to suggest CV-CV-CV spellings of words—that is, spellings that suggest the regular alternation of consonants and vowels—that do not always match the way words are actually spoken. In one sense, then, the syllabary provides a surplus of linguistic information—extra vowels. In another sense it provides a deficit: some key knowledge necessary to read a word correctly is missing. One might alternatively say that the syllabary simultaneously undercodes and overcodes the spoken language, making it particularly ripe as a location for local language ideology.

Therefore, I was surprised to learn of a set of beliefs that attributed to the syllabary a kind of authority in terms of pronunciation—in short, a belief in a "literate" pronunciation of Cherokee. A number of speakers saw the written (syllabic) version of a word and the CV-CV-CV pronunciations it implies as being "correct," and saw the normally spoken version of that word as being "colloquial." One of my consultants said that for words where there is such a difference in the written and spoken versions, there is a "syllabary" pronunciation and a "local" (by implication, oral) pronunciation. This belief in a "syllabary" pronunciation is not unlike the belief in spelling pronunciation in English that causes people to pronounce the /r/ in "February" with special care when they are reading aloud or otherwise speaking formally. However, unless the circumstances call for extremely heightened self-consciousness, syllabary pronunciations were usually not uttered, even in careful speech, by most fluent speakers of Cherokee.[1]

As an example, I will use the Cherokee word for apple, *sv:ktha*. The consonant cluster /kt/ is impossible to represent using the syllabary; therefore, a character containing the consonant /k/ *and* a vowel must be used. By convention,[2] the word is spelled ⟨ᏒᎦᏔ⟩ in the syllabary. A "literate" pronunciation of this word would therefore be *sv:kahtha*. Of all the consultants I asked about this example, not one indicated that he or she would actually say *sv:kahta* in speaking. Nevertheless, there remained on the part of many of the speakers I interviewed a belief that this type of pronunciation has some authenticity or value. Speakers especially seemed to feel that this pronunciation would be accurate if one were reading aloud. Again, one is reminded of the goal one is urged to approach in reading English—reading every letter on the page.

One consultant told me that the full "syllabary" pronunciations are correct, while at the same time he acknowledged that such pronunciations would not be understood by other speakers:

> Okay. Here's a good one. Like a meeting, like the people are going to meet. . . . I'll say *ha:ntsosgoʔi*, okay. But then you go somewhere else and you read that word . . . —the syllable for *ha*, or the one for *na* to represent a group. Some people use *ahni* or *tsu:ni* to indicate more than one, a group. Here is the problem. Correctly, the way it's written in the Cherokee Testament, it is *a:nitsohsgoʔi*, is to meet. But people around here say *da:ntsohsgoʔi*. See they leave that a sound off of that n. They just borrow the n from the *na* sound, the *na*, and just borrow the n and just say *da:ntsohsgoʔi*. Where if it's written it would be *danahtsohsgoʔi*. And some people say *danahtsohsgoʔi* but most of them say *ha:ntsohsgoʔi*. That's the slang right there. Properly, the way it's written sounds correct: *danahtsohsgoʔi*. But when you say that people don't know what you're saying. You know, it's just like, huh?

Some consultants told me that learning correct pronunciations was a major motivation in their learning the syllabary. I heard that learning and preserving the writing system is an important step toward keeping the language from deteriorating. This view of spoken language as ephemeral and written language as permanent is certainly not limited to native perceptions of the Cherokee language. However, the idea that writing is a rigid codification of what otherwise might be lost may be traceable, at least in part, to events of the early nineteenth century. The near simultaneity of the syllabary's invention, adoption, use in the codification of Cherokee law and government, usage by medicine men to record formulas, and the Cherokees' tragic removal may have underscored, for this particular language community, the value of having things written down. (On the other hand, it might have underscored the futility of writing things down.) Raymond D. Fogelson has noted that the syllabary may be seen as having reified Cherokee medicine and magic.

> After the 1838 Removal and the invention of the Sequoyah syllabary, conjuring and medical practices tended to lose much of their former flexibility and assumed a more rigid, doctrinaire quality among the remaining Eastern Cherokee. . . . The syllabary enabled the Eastern Cherokee to set down and retain much tribal knowledge, but this new device seems also to have affected some of the flexible spirit pervading the earlier medicine and conjuring. The ability to write down prayers, incantations, and formulae in notebooks gave these items a certain tangibility that grew into reverence. The conjuror's notebook became imbued with some of the same holiness surrounding the white man's Bible (Fogelson 1980: 61–62).

Note that it is only Cherokee *attitudes* and *practices* concerning the new texts that could cause this increase in rigidity; written texts can be modified and replaced when attitudes permit. The syllabary's perceived rigidity, then, and its perceived usefulness as a tool of language preservation reflect a powerful language ideology.

Why is there such reverence for this writing system on the part of speakers, I wondered, when linguists and historians have been so quick to point out its flaws? Here appears a puzzling contradiction; it is not because of native unawareness of the syllabary's limitations. Indeed, one of the chief rationales for using the international or "linguist's" phonetic system described in the last chapter is that it supplies information missing from syllabic writing. This system, as the reader will recall, includes representation of the glottal stop, vowel length, pitch, and intrusive h, which easy and standard phonetics generally do not. It also differs in the writing of some consonants.

Other native users of the syllabary, besides linguistically trained language teachers, have sought remedies for its shortcomings as well. It was apparently not uncommon at one time for medicine men and others to mark their characters idiosyncratically so as to make distinctions, omitted by Sequoyah, that they found necessary. Teacher B demonstrated three such distinctions that he had learned from a Cherokee preacher who helped him learn the language. ⟨S⟩, /thu/, was distinguished from ⟨S⟩, /tu/; ⟨Λ⟩, /tho/, from ⟨V⟩, /to/; and ⟨ᴄᴏ⟩, /thv/, from ⟨ᴏᴏ⟩, /tv/.

Such modifications to the syllabary, which would narrow it as a system of transcription (that is, would make it more detailed in its representation of spoken Cherokee), would mainly interest writers rather than readers. The New Testament and other sources of written Cherokee use only the unmodified Sequoyan system. For the kind of reading most literate Cherokees now do, therefore, these idiosyncratic modifications are of no practical use. That may be why I encountered no other consultants who used or even knew of such modifications. But language teachers, who generally were aware of the syllabary's representational deficiencies, never practiced or suggested such modifications of the syllabary either; instead, they relied on an entirely separate orthography as an alternative or supplement. The syllabary itself was never changed.

Ironically, in spite of this native awareness of the shortcomings of the syllabary, it was still seen as an authoritative source of linguistic knowledge. This may in part be explained by the understood history of the syllabary, its inventor, and its role in the relationship between Eastern and Western Cherokees. Because Sequoyah spoke what linguists and Cherokees generally call the "Overhill" dialect, the syllabary is considered to reflect that dialect more closely than it does Eastern ones.[3] This dialect is held to be much more commonly spoken in Oklahoma than in North Carolina. In fact, North Carolina speakers familiar with the term "Overhill" would be likely to say that that dialect is or has become the "Oklahoma" or "Western" dialect. Residents of Snowbird, the small Cherokee community fifty or so miles to the southwest of Cherokee, are believed to speak a dialect much closer to this Western dialect than do residents of Cherokee itself. Raymond D. Fogelson (pers. com., May 1995) has suggested that the Snowbird dialect is a survival of Valley dialect, now spoken in some parts of Oklahoma. King (1975) considers Snowbird as a fourth dialect, distinct from the Middle, Overhill, and Lower (now extinct) dialects. The Snowbird dialect, according to King, "superficially at least, . . . seems to represent a mixing of elements from the Overhill and Middle dialects. This may have resulted in part from residence before removal in an area contiguous to both of the major dialects" (1975: 10).

This belief, that the syllabary reflects a Western or Oklahoman way of speaking, may lend a kind of ironic or bittersweet authority to the syllabary. For although Cherokee, North Carolina, is considered to be the "homeland," and is called *tsa:la:ki uwe:thi*, Old or Ancient Cherokee, by Oklahoma Cherokees, some seem to feel, on both sides of the divide, that the most authentic Cherokee culture and language went west on the Trail of Tears. As Fogelson has noted, "Besides throwing the culture into a state of generalized confusion, the removal isolated the Eastern Cherokee from the creative leadership, which had done so much to elevate their Nation to a civilized status. Also among the 18,000 or so who emigrated west were probably many conjurors of high repute, as well as other guardians of traditional belief" (1980: 62).

Not everyone in the Eastern Cherokee community agreed, however, that the Cherokees' creative leadership, or more specifically, their linguistic authority, moved west along the Trail of Tears. Some consultants suggested that the dialectal differences between East and West resulted from the long separation, everyone having "talked the same" before removal. One elderly traditionalist told me that the Oklahoma dialect is "mixed with Creek." A Snowbird resident told me that the Western Cherokees had lost some of their lexical items along the way. Specifically, he referred to the much disputed word for 'thank you,' which is *ski* for most Eastern speakers, and *wa?to* for Western speakers. "We say *ski* for thank you, and *wa?to* [means] you're welcome. So I asked [an Oklahoma speaker], what do they say for you're welcome? He didn't know! So he must 'a' lost it somewhere along the trail there. We speak the right way, from here, you know, cause it started from here, you know. [They] might have forgotten when they was driven out of here."

In contrast, a number of consultants expressed the belief that Oklahoma Cherokee is "right," that it is fuller or more complete than the Cherokee spoken in North Carolina. The following conversation I had with an elderly Snowbird resident, former Cherokee language teacher and social service worker, suggests that both Oklahoma speech and biblical writing are seen as fuller and more prestigious than everyday Eastern speech.

Consultant: [In] plain speaking you don't need the Bible. You need the Bible for the churches, something like that.

MB: What are some of the differences between the Cherokee in the Bible and the Cherokee that you speak every day?

Consultant: That, I don't know how to explain it to you. Just like you know, talk[ing] about the churches, *ti:kalawihstihi.* We don't use that everyday, I mean, we do if we [are] going to Sunday, or something, or if we asked somebody to go to church, we'll use that, but other than that—and just like where it says *ti* and *a* and stuff like that, we don't use all of that, everyday speaking.

MB: I've heard from some people that the Bible's written closer to the way that people in Oklahoma speak. Do you find that?

Consultant: Yeah. It is. They use a lot of that, you know. They're into the—almost of what the Bible speaks of, the way they speaks. And we speaks just more plain like. Take northern people or South people. South people, they speak the way they want to speak. And the northern people it's kind of more of a—how would you say it, more classy pronouncing.

MB: So you think the Oklahoma speakers are more classy?

Consultant: Yeah.

The fact that the syllabary is seen as closely representing Oklahoma speech served for people like adult language Teacher E both as authentication for that dialect and also as authentication of written (syllabic) Cherokee, such as that found in the New Testament.

The implications of the notion that Oklahoma speech and the New Testament have in common a close relationship with the syllabary have not been lost on members of the community. One woman, a non-Indian and nonspeaker but longtime member of the Cherokee community, told me that Oklahoma Cherokee was like "the King's English." This parallel was quite astute, because many Cherokees believe their translation of the New Testament to be analogous to, and directly translated from, the King James Bible. Oklahoma Cherokee, which North Carolina speakers tend to equate with the written Cherokee of the New Testament, is therefore like the King's English, indeed!

The Bible serves as a kind of stand-in for an Eastern dictionary and grammar, in that it is considered an authoritative written model and source for lexical items, and it is certainly the largest single body of Cherokee text anywhere available. This means that the best and most complete source of information about and in Cherokee sylla-bary is inextricably religious in nature. This can have quite a seri-ous impact on a speaker's relationship to the written Cherokee word, and sheds some light on the reverence for syllabary that I described above. While some speakers I talked to felt free as they read from the New Testament to pronounce words differently from the way they are spelled (for example, omitting unidiomatic vowels or altering conso-nants to reflect their own dialect), some did not. One consultant ex-plained that what is written in the Bible cannot be changed, meaning thereby that it should not be mispronounced.[4] This trend resulted in two phenomena: (1) speakers reading aloud consonants or even lexi-cal items that they would never utter in their own dialect in normal speech, and (2) speakers adding in vowels they would not pronounce in other contexts, delivering the "syllabary" pronunciation I mentioned earlier. I asked a Snowbird elder about the first sort of substitution: "I've heard that some people, when they're reading the Bible, when they come across something like *hatlv,* they'll translate it to *katsv,* sort of without even thinking about it. But you try not to do that." (*Ha:tlv* is the word for 'where' used in the Bible and by most Oklahoma speakers; *ka:tsv* is the word for 'where' used by most North Carolina speakers.) She answered, "Yes. I try not to do that. Even though . . . I'm afraid I'm gonna slip. And Mama said always stick to your learnings."

These pronunciations were seen by some of my consultants as re-flecting religious devotion more than dialect. A respected Snowbird elder told me that Snowbird dialect was probably closer to the lan-guage represented in the Bible than was the dialect spoken on the Boundary because "they's more Indian Bible readers here in this com-munity!" According to this argument, the piety of the Snowbird com-munity, rather than historical circumstance, has kept its dialect in line with the New Testament. Another Snowbird consultant argued that Western Cherokees who studied their Bibles were more likely to speak like Snowbird residents.

MB: Do you think one of the dialects, here or in Oklahoma, is most correct?

Snowbird consultant: [Long pause.] Well, Oklahoma people are some of us. And I would have to say that I do not hear Oklahoma that much. But the ones that really have read their Cherokee are pretty much as in my area.

MB: The ones that have read Cherokee.

Snowbird consultant: Uh-huh, the ones that have read the Cherokee. And those that have somebody to teach them, I think.

MB: So . . . is it just that [the people that read Cherokee are] the most similar to each other, or do they speak more correctly than others?

Snowbird consultant: They speak more correctly, yeah, you know. Those that can read Cherokee. Let's say the Testament, let's put it that way.

For some consultants, then, Oklahoma speech was seen as more "correct" only to the degree that it reflects biblical pronunciations. Raymond Fogelson (pers. com., May 1995) suggested, furthermore, that Oklahoma speech may *not* be seen as the standard where the writing of *itikewesti*, Cherokee medicinal texts, is concerned. As he points out, the Eastern homeland is the source for most of the plants, animals, and features of the landscape called upon in these traditional ceremonies. Although I do not have sufficient data on this to draw any conclusions, I will note that the reasons consultants generally gave for notebooks being hard to read is that they were written idiosyncratically and secretively, rather than that they reflected an unfamiliar dialect. Medicinal texts might then be a potential source of writing that is *not* strongly associated with Western speech.

Generally, then, the triadic association of Oklahoma speech, biblical writing, and correctness is strong in local language ideology and practice. But in the mid-1990s, there was an opposite trend standing in tension with this one. There was a movement among some North Carolina speakers to define, preserve, and authenticate their *own* dialect. As the reader is by now aware, most of the printed material available in the Cherokee syllabary and both the most widely available Cherokee language textbook and dictionary are oriented toward speakers from Oklahoma. In what was partially a response to that state of affairs, the eldest member of one prominent family in Cherokee started a project to preserve, teach, and produce materials in what he considered to be the most correct, most characteristically Eastern, and, one might say, the standard of the Eastern dialects. This respected speaker has also served as a linguistic consultant to numerous linguists and other scholars. This group referred to their dialect as *kituhwa,* a term generally used in the Cherokee language literature to refer to the Cherokee spoken by today's Qualla Boundary residents as a whole. This group, however, used the term to designate what they saw as a more specific dialect—an Eastern standard—possibly with origins in the ancient Cherokee town of *kituhwa.*[5]

The group's core members were mostly elderly, Cherokee-speaking members of the community, although some nonspeaking community residents participated in important capacities. A belief in the importance of this dialect preservation effort and, hence, an implicit acknowledgment of the dialect itself came to be shared by the (largely nonspeaking) community at large as well. This organization was entrusted by the Eastern Band with the task of creating new curricular materials that reflected this specific dialect. In keeping with the group's priorities, the dialect spoken by applicants was a serious consideration in hiring Cherokee language teachers in those years. Because there were comparatively few fluent speakers from the central part of the reservation, one new teacher hired in 1993 was from Oklahoma and the other was from the Snowbird community, where residents were not considered to speak the *kituhwa* dialect. Though hired, they were instructed to learn the *kituhwa* dialect and to use it in their classes.

Through the project, speakers and nonspeakers were brought together as a community not primarily via language use itself but by means of a set of beliefs about language use. This would-be North Carolina standard and the speech community it suggested iconically represented a certain vision of the structure of the social community; its source was considered to be located near the center of the present-day Cherokee community, and the evidence for it was considered to weaken as one moved toward the periphery. The assertion of this pure Eastern dialectal "core" may be seen as an iconic representation of the cultural integrity and internal structure of the Eastern Cherokee more generally, a valuable assertion in the face of the tourist onslaught and competition from Oklahoma.

Although some members of this project took very seriously the notion of "syllabary" pronunciation, they also acknowledged the proximity of syllabary spellings, particularly in the New Testament and hymnal, to the Oklahoma speech that they were trying to reject as a standard. This meant that, for example, hymns from the hymnal were rewritten in syllabary to reflect local dialectal pronunciations. ⟨Ꮈ⟩, *tlha*, 'not,' was rewritten ⟨Ꮬ⟩, *tsa*, for example.[6] The project was attempting, then, to sever the bond between Oklahoma speech and the syllabary, while maintaining—in fact, while insisting upon the necessity of—the syllabary's link to some standard, however defined.

At one meeting of the project, photocopied sheets bearing Cherokee Hymn 86, "I Would Not Live Always," were handed out.[7] These pages contained all five verses of the hymn written out by hand, first in syllabary and then in international phonetics. Each page had two versions of both the syllabary verses and the phonetic ones; on the front were the *kituhwa* versions, and on the back, the Western versions. Despite the fact that there were few differences, each version was written out in its entirety. Most of the differences involved the dialectal changes of /tlh/ or /tl/ to /tsh/ or /ts/. The first line, for example, 'I would not live always,' was ⟨Ꮦꭳꭰꮈ hᎪꭴꮙᎢ ꭴꭲꭱꭳꮈ⟩ in the *kituhwa* version with phonetics given as "Thseʔsti nikohi:lv: ʔi yikeʔe:sti," and ⟨Ꮅꭳꮈ hᎪꭴꮙᎢ ꭴꭲꭱꭳꮈ⟩ in the Western version with "Tleʔsti nikohilv: ʔi yikeʔe:sti" written as the phonetics. One elder specifically noted that while some argue that the spellings and pronunciations reflected in the Bible must be the only right ones, this was not so!

There was another possible way to deal with this dilemma, exemplified by a number of North Carolina Cherokee New Testament readers. That is, they treated the syllabary as a standard in the sense that, while the syllabic writing itself does not change, readers are free to pronounce words according to their own dialectal background. A reader following this practice might see the word ⟨ꭲꮈ⟩, *vthla*, 'no,' on the page and read out *v:tsha* or even *kehsti*. The first case (reading *v:tsha*) would be similar to an American speaker of English seeing the word "isn't" on a page and pronouncing it "idn't," according to his or her dialect. The second (substituting *kehsti* for *v:tlha* in reading) would be as if the English reader substituted ain't—a different lexical form altogether— for isn't.

But for those who maintained the syllabary's link with a correct, "literate" pronunciation of some kind, there was still a problem— namely, that the syllabary leaves huge orthographic gaps, in terms of vowel length and so on, as discussed earlier. There was thus an irre-solvable tension in this movement to establish an Eastern standard with its own "syllabary" spellings and pronunciations. The supplemen-tal information provided by the syllabary, the extra vowels, had to be considered significant and, indeed, correct. At the same time, steps had to be taken to fill in the syllabary's gaps through simultaneous use of international phonetics. The principles of international phonetics were then even applied to the fictitious complete syllables suggested by syllabic writing. For example, when, earlier in the chapter, I wrote the word 'apple,' normally pronounced *sv:ktha*, as ⟨sv:kahtha⟩, I was writing the three syllables (ᏘᏍᏩ) in the way they would have to be pro-nounced according to the patterns of spoken Cherokee, if they were all fully pronounced. The character ⟨Ᏻ⟩ (/ka/) contains no information about aspiration following the vowel, but I wrote it with an ⟨h⟩ be-cause that is how it would have to be pronounced, according to the phonological rules of Cherokee, in order to precede /tha/. In ordinary speech, however, the second vowel never would be pronounced. This practice, which I learned from working with the language preserva-tion and education group, suggests a reality to the full middle syllable that it simply does not have in spoken Cherokee. Over time, this prac-tice could influence the common pronunciations of words, as books replace elderly speakers as sources of linguistic information.

This tension, between the syllabary's perceived correctness and its perceived incompleteness, became quite apparent when one member of the group suggested removing *all* international phonetic modifi-cations (such as aspiration, vowel length, and so on) from syllabary spellings, like ⟨sv:kahtha⟩, since those modifications do not exist in the syllabary. *All* such modifications were to be removed, even if they *did* accurately represent aspects of a spoken word. A major objective of providing syllabary spellings, however, had been to provide the fullest, most complete, and most correct pronunciation possible.

Most speakers acknowledged that one did not have to be conver-sant with the syllabary in order to be a fluent speaker of the Cherokee language. However, knowledge of the syllabary was seen as being an extremely important component of one's overall linguistic proficiency, and I cannot think of anyone in the Cherokee community who was called upon as an "expert" in linguistic matters who did not read syllabary.[8] Although it was acknowledged on some level, then, that the syllabary is a writing system and not an integral part of the Cherokee language itself, the syllabary was on another level seen as being inextricably bound to the Cherokee language, and as far from being arbitrary as one can imagine. This inherent relationship between the syllabary and certain kinds of meaning works iconically, in that the syllabary "looks like" Cherokee, and it also works indexically, in that the syllabary is a crucial marker of authenticity and authority.

Most of my consultants did not seem to have reflected on the mechanics of the syllabary, or on the ways in which it differs from an alphabet. That is, most would not articulate the difference as being one between the representation of cv units and the representation of c or v units. One consultant joked, "Well, you can't write French with [the syllabary]." Of course, to write French with the syllabary would require some phonological compromises. But that is exactly what happens every day, as words move from one language to another, from one orthography to another. I got little sense from my consultants that such movement was considered possible where the syllabary was concerned, or that the syllabary was considered to be an arbitrary representation of sounds like any other writing system.

Words that are borrowed into Cherokee and given a syllabary spelling tend, therefore, to retain the resultant syllabary "spelling" pronunciation, rather than being read as English words. Probably the most famous example of this tendency is the name of the legendary Cherokee martyr, *Tsa:li*. This man's Anglo name was Charley, but the syllabary approximation of that English name, ⟨GⱣ⟩, would be pronounced as *Tsa:li* by most North Carolina speakers. The idea that the syllabary could be used to write English words, or words from any other language, with some phonological mismatch, was not overtly recognized by the people with whom I spoke.

The notion that the syllabary's graphemic signs arbitrarily represent sounds instead of specifically coding Cherokee syllables was not generally present among the operating Cherokee ideologies of literacy I encountered. Clearly, this belief about the syllabary differed from local beliefs about the writing of English, since the phenomenon of easy phonetics rested entirely on the underlying notion that "English" spellings may easily be transferred from the representation of one language to another. The other forms of phonetic writing were also seen as representing sounds, not specifically the Cherokee language. This can be seen in the fact that, for example, the international phonetic system was rejected by some speakers because they believed that it represented the *wrong* sounds, and, by implication, standard phonetics represented the right ones.[9] Foregrounded about the syllabary, then, and setting it apart from other local writing systems were its non-arbitrary, nonsymbolic dimensions. As far from being arbitrary as was possible, the syllabary was treated as though it had a direct, tangible connection to meaning.

In the children's classrooms, it would certainly have been possible to introduce an activity that asked children to draw on the phonetic values of the syllabary characters to write the English language, but this was never done. I also never observed students doing this spontaneously as a way to build on the code potential of the syllabary. The point is that because the syllabary serves at least in part as a culturally specific code, it cannot also be an arbitrary phonetic writing system with fixed phonetic, but no fixed semantic, meanings. Since the syllabary is a code, every piece of it has to *mean something*. As mentioned in the previous chapter, one consultant told me that her ability to read and write syllabary was limited because she did not "understand" all the characters. The choice of the word "understand," as opposed to, for example, "know," is significant because it suggests that each character has a meaning. It is at this juncture that the articulated and unarticulated beliefs about the syllabary come together. This consultant's reverence for the syllabary and her statement suggesting that it is something to be *understood* rely heavily on the presuppositions of in-group, nonphonetic codeness of the syllabary discussed in Chapter 3.

The idea that the syllables are actually syllable-long morphemes with stable semantic meanings is suggested by three Cherokee cultural phenomena.[10] These are (1) the importance of presenting the characters in a particular structure, especially when learning their values, whether that structure be the original Sequoyan order, Worcester's chart, or John 1 (see Figure 8); (2) the rebuslike interpretations of some of the characters as *shapes* that are *English* puns on the syllables they represent in the Sequoyan system; and (3) the practice of trying to find a morphological or semantic justification for the otherwise arbitrary

ᎣᏍᏛ ᎧᏃᎮᏛ, ᏣᏂ ᎤᏬᏪᎳᏅᎯ.

ᎠᏯᏙᎸᎢ 1

1 ᏗᏓᎴᏂᏍᎬ ᎧᏃᎮᏛ ᎡᎮᎢ, ᎠᎴ
ᎾᏍᎩ ᎧᏃᎮᏛ ᎤᏁᎳᏅᎯ ᎢᏧᎳᎭ Ꭰ-
ᏁᎮᎢ, ᎠᎴ ᎾᏍᎩ ᎧᏃᎮᏛ ᎤᏁᎳᏅᎯ
ᎨᏎᎢ.
2 ᏗᏓᎴᏂᏍᎬᎢ ᎾᏍᎩ ᎤᏁᎳᏅᎯ
ᎢᏧᎳᎭ ᎠᏁᎮᎢ.
3 ᏂᎦᎥ ᎪᎱᏍᏗ ᎾᏍᎩ ᎤᏬᏢᏁᎢ, ᎠᎴ
ᏂᎦᎥ ᎪᏢᏅᎯ ᏥᎩ ᎥᏝ ᎪᎱᏍᏗ ᎾᏍᎩ
ᏄᏬᏢᏅᎾ ᏱᎩ.
4 ᎾᏍᎩ [ᎧᏃᎮᏛ] ᎬᏂᏛ ᎤᏪᎮᎢ;
ᎠᎴ ᎾᏍᎩ ᎬᏂᏛ ᏴᏫ ᎢᎦ ᎤᎾᏘᏍᏓᏁᎯ
ᎨᏎᎢ.
5 ᎠᎴ ᎾᏍᎩ ᎢᎦ-ᎦᏘᏍᏗᏍᎩ ᎤᎵᏏᎬ
ᏚᏄᏌᏕᎢ, ᎤᎵᏏᎩᏃ ᎥᏝ ᏱᏚᏏᏂᎸᏤᎢ.
6 ᎩᎶ ᎢᏳᏍᏗ ᎠᏍᎦᏯ ᎡᎲᎩ ᏣᏂ
ᏧᏙᎢᏛ ᎤᏁᎳᏅᎯ ᏅᏓᏳᏅᏏᏛ ᎨᏒᎩ.
7 ᎾᏍᎩ ᎤᎷᏨᎩ ᎧᏃᎮᏍᎩ ᎨᏒᎩ,
ᎾᏍᎩ ᎢᎦ-ᎦᏘ ᎤᏃᎮᏗᏱ, ᎾᏍᎩ ᎢᏳ-
ᏩᏂᏐᏗᏱ ᎾᏂᎥ ᎤᏃᎯᏳᏗᏱ.
8 ᎥᏝ ᎾᏍᎩ Ꮎ ᎢᎦ-ᎦᏘ ᏱᎨᏎᎢ, Ꭷ-
ᏃᎮᏍᎩᏉᏍᎩᏂ ᎨᏒᎩ ᎾᏍᎩ ᎢᎦ-ᎦᏘ.
9 ᎾᏍᎩᏍᎩᏂ Ꮎ ᎧᏃᎮᏛ ᎤᏙᎯᏳᏒ
ᎢᎦ-ᎦᏘ ᎨᏒᎩ; ᎾᏍᎩ ᎡᎶᎯ ᏗᎷᏨ,
ᎢᎦ ᏥᏕᎠᏘᏍᏓᏁ ᎾᏂᎥ ᏴᏫ.
10 ᎾᏍᎩ ᎡᎶᎯ ᎡᎲᎩ, ᎠᎴ ᎾᏍᎩ
ᎡᎶᎯ ᎤᏬᏢᏅᎯ ᎨᏒᎩ, ᎠᎴ ᎡᎶᎯ ᎥᏝ
ᏳᏬᎵᏤᎢ.
11 ᎤᏤᎵᎪᎯ ᎤᎷᏨᎩ, ᎠᏎᏃ ᏧᏤᎵ
ᎥᏝ ᏱᏗᎬᏩᏓᏂᎸᏤᎢ.
12 ᎾᏂᎥᏍᎩᏂ ᏗᎬᏩᏓᏂᎸᏨᎯ ᏕᎤ-
ᎵᏍᎪᎸᏓᏁᎸᎩ ᎤᏁᎳᏅᎯ ᏧᏪᏥ Ꭲ-
ᏳᎾᎵᏍᏙᏗᏱ; ᎾᏍᎩ ᏕᎤᏙᎥ ᎠᏃᎯᏳ-
ᎲᏍᎩ;
13 ᎾᏍᎩ ᎩᎬ ᏗᎾᏄᎪᏫᏒᎯ ᏂᎨᏒᎾ,
ᎠᎴ ᎤᏇᏓᎵ ᎠᏓᏅᏖᏍᎬ ᏗᎾᏄᎪᏫᏒᎯ
ᏂᎨᏒᎾ, ᎠᎴ ᏴᏫ ᎠᏓᏅᏖᏍᎬ ᏗᎾᏄ-
ᎪᏫᏒᎯ ᏂᎨᏒᎾ, ᎤᏁᎳᏅᎯᏍᎩᏂ ᏗᎾᏄ-
ᎪᏫᏒᎯ.
14 ᎠᎴ ᎧᏃᎮᏛ ᎤᏇᏓᎵ ᏄᎵᏍᏔ-
ᏅᎩ, ᎠᎴ ᎢᏕᎲ ᎤᎴᏂᏙᎸᎩ, ᎤᎧᎵᏨᎯ
ᎨᏒᎩ ᎤᏓᏙᎵᏣᏛ ᎠᎴ ᏚᏳᎪᏛᎢ; ᎠᎴ
ᎢᏗᎪᏩᏘᏍᎬᎩ ᎤᏤᎵᎦ ᎦᎸᏉᏗᏳ Ꭸ-
ᏒᎢ, ᎾᏍᎩ ᎦᎸᏉᏗᏳ ᎨᏒ ᎠᎦᏴᎵᎨ
ᎤᏩᏒᎯᏳ ᎤᏕᏁᎸᎯ ᎤᏤᎵᎦ ᎾᏍᎩᏯ
ᎨᏒᎩ.
15 ᏣᏂ ᎧᏃᎮᏍᎬᎩ ᎾᏍᎩ [ᎧᏃᎮᏛ,]
ᎠᎴ ᎤᏪᎷᏅᎩ ᎯᎠ ᏄᏪᏒᎩ; ᎯᎠ
ᎾᏍᎩ ᏥᏥᏃᎮᏍᎬᎩ, ᎯᎠ ᏥᏂᏥᏪ-
ᏍᎬᎩ, ᎣᏂ ᏨᏓᏯᎢ ᎢᎬᏱ ᎠᎦᎴᏗ,
ᎾᏍᎩᏰᏃ ᎡᎲᎩ ᎠᏏ ᏂᎨᎥᎾ ᏥᎨᏒᎩ.
16 ᎠᎴ ᎾᏍᎩ ᎤᎧᎵᏨᎯ ᎨᏒ ᏂᏗᎥ
ᎡᎩᏁᎸᎯ, ᎬᏩᎦᏘᏯᏰᏃ ᎤᏓᏙᎵᏍᏗ
ᎨᏒ ᎤᎶᏏᎶᏛ ᎡᎩᏁᎸ.
17 ᏗᎧᎿᏩᏛᏍᏗᏰᏃ ᎼᏏ ᎬᏂᎨᏒ
ᎢᏳᏩᏁᎸᎯ ᎨᏒᎩ, ᎤᏓᏙᎵᏣᏛᏍᎩᏂ
ᎠᎴ ᏚᏳᎪᏛᎢ ᏥᏌ ᎦᎶᏁᏛ ᏂᏙᏓᏳᎵ-
ᏍᎪᎸᏔᏅᎯ.
18 ᎥᏝ ᎩᎶ ᎢᎸᎯᏳ ᏱᎬᏩᎪᎨ ᎤᏁ-
ᎳᏅᎯ; ᎤᏩᏒᎯᏳ ᎤᏕᏁᎸᎯ ᎤᏪᏥ,
ᎠᎦᏴᎵᎨ ᎦᏁᏥᎢ ᎡᎯ, ᎾᏍᎩ ᎬᏂᎨᏒ
ᏄᏩᏁᎸ.
19 ᎠᎴ ᎾᏍᎩ ᎯᎠ ᏣᏂ ᎤᏃᎮᎸᎯ,
ᎾᎯᏳ ᎠᏂᏧᏏ ᏥᎷᏏᎵᎻ ᏙᏧᏂᏅᏒ
ᎠᏥᎸ-ᎠᏁᎶᎯ ᎠᎴ ᎠᏂᎵᏫ ᎬᏩᏛᏛ-
ᏗᏱ, ᎯᎠ ᎢᏳᏂᏪᏍᏗᏱ; ᎦᎪ ᏂᎯ?
20 ᎠᎴ Ꭴ‘ᏃᏅᎩ, ᎠᎴ ᎥᏝ ᏳᏓᏱᎴᎢ,
Ꭴ‘ᏃᏅᏉᏍᎩᏂ ᎯᎠ ᏄᏪᏒᎩ; ᎥᏝ ᎠᏴ
ᎦᎶᏁᏛ ᏱᎩ.

Figure 8. John 1 from the Cherokee New Testament.

choice of syllabary characters in consonant clusters. Each of these phenomena merits a closer look.

As I noted earlier, the popular chart providing students of the syllabary with phonetic spellings is arranged for the benefit of speakers of English. Certainly, it is of no value to people who do not read some European language or who are unfamiliar with the Latin alphabet. The many Cherokees, Sequoyah included, who never read English used another method for organizing and memorizing the values of the syllabary characters well into this century. Sequoyah always wrote the characters out in the same order,[11] an order that was later used by Cherokee traditionalist Will West Long,[12] and which is reproduced even today on pottery and, until it closed, on the Sequoyah Cafeteria sign in downtown Cherokee. It stands to reason that there is a mnemonic pattern structuring this ordered list, but I have not been able to ascertain what it is.[13] It may be lost. But the possibility of such a pattern suggests that, from its inception, the syllabary was introduced to Cherokee speakers by means of a specific content to be associated with each character.

I spoke to a number of literate community members about this order, and not one told me that he or she learned the characters in this order or ever used the order in any mnemonic way. In fact, most seemed startled when I pointed out that both Sequoyah and Will West Long used an order different from the familiar chart. However, it is significant that the order continues to make its way into the presentation of the syllabary in designed artifacts produced for tourism.

If the original Sequoyan order had any semantic or poetic mnemonic functions, it seems possible that these two functions have diverged and are now fulfilled by two separate texts. The New Testament, and particularly John 1, provide a semantic base for some syllabary learners, while the phonetic chart itself serves a poetic function.

Many beginners told me that they used John 1 when they first learned the syllabary. I met one Cherokee woman who could deliver a reading of the first few verses that made her seem a quite fluent reader. As soon as she moved away from this text, however, her apparent reading skills dissipated. It was evident that she had learned these first few verses by heart and hoped, by reciting them while following along in the syllabary New Testament, to master the syllabary characters themselves.

I asked Teacher B, the local preacher and syllabary teacher, what part of the New Testament he turned to in learning the syllabary.

Teacher B: Any place is as good as another. Really, in the Gospel of John, I guess. [Because] I had two years of Greek, and they said that, you know, the best place to study language [is the] Gospel of John. I may have turned to that.

MB: Why is that? Where does that come from? I mean I've heard a lot of people say that, that they start with John, and I just wondered—

Teacher B: I don't know. Way God set it up, I guess.

I heard two other theories offered as to why learners use this particular text. Some argued that it is easy, because the same words (and characters) occur repetitively throughout the text. Adult language Teacher E subscribed to this view.

Teacher E: Yeah, well the Book of John, there, that's about one of the easiest ones to learn because there are so many words in . . . the first verse there, there's the one word in there, the word, 'word,' it's in there twice, just in that one verse.

MB: Khanoheta?

Teacher E: Yeah, uh-huh. And that's the easiest way of learning it, if you see it twice, and even the second verse still has that, and you can recognize it by looking at it, you know you've seen it here, in the first verse, and it's in the second verse, so you'll know what that is. I've learned that pretty fast. First and second, and, well, my aunt told me about this, and it was true, that you could learn that easy.

MB: And is it mainly the repetition . . . ?

Teacher E: It probably is, because you can see the word again, and you remember what it is. I started with Matthew myself, and it took me a while just to get two or three words.

An elderly Yellowhill resident confirmed the view that John is the easiest Gospel.

MB: When you were teaching yourself, why did you choose John?

YR: I don't know, he's about the easiest, I guess, to learn. I believe it is. I know a lot of 'em that says, they're trying to read Cherokee, says, read John, read that, says that's the easiest. It says, *titale:niska ehe:ʔi* ['in the beginning'].

Others suggested what is basically the opposite argument—that John is the best to use because virtually all the characters are contained there, and so a person could learn the whole system by learning this small bit of text. If so, how close this would be to a meaningful mnemonic! It is also significant that John 1 links the beginning, the Word, and God—inspiring to the Christian who is trying to learn to read the Bible in his or her native tongue.

I discussed the original Sequoyan order, contrasting it with Worcester's chart, with a public school Cherokee language and Sunday school teacher. He immediately began looking for parallels to the New Testament. He told me he was unfamiliar with the arrangement, but I asked him if it seemed to him to make any sense or to have any meaning. When he read aloud the first two characters of Sequoyah's list, ⟨R, D⟩, /e/, /a/, he said that it almost makes a word, like one found on the first page of the New Testament, which he promptly went to get. Returning, he showed me the first word on the first page. It was ⟨ᎯD⟩, *hiʔa.* He scanned Sequoyah's arrangements, looking for more biblical words. ⟨ᏫᏪᏢᏁᎯᏥ⟩, /wu/ /we/ /tlv/ /ne/ /hi/ /ki/, he pronounced as *uwe:tlanv hiki,* stretching his reading of the characters to make the word 'God.' Some of the characters do seem to come together to make words, he said, but then they "drop off." There might or might not be a meaning, he concluded.

He was not unresponsive, then, to the possibility that the pre-chart order had a meaning, a hidden message, that made it possible to remember and reproduce. But it must unquestionably, in his view, be a biblical message. This is nearly impossible, because Sequoyah's development of the syllabary in its original order predated both the system's use to translate the Bible and the widespread conversion of the Cherokees. This reflex, however, suggests a pattern of looking for recognizable biblical meanings and words in unknown syllabary text, or of using knowledge of biblical content to assist in the mechanics of linking up syllabary text with spoken words. Thus reading the *Bible* seemed to be the default mode of reading *syllabary.*

If the New Testament has come to provide the semantic mnemonic

Characters	Ꮮ	Ꮈ
Syllable represented	/le/	/lu/
Sounds like English word	lay	Lou
Mnemonic	Figure "laying" down (head down, feet up)	First letter of English name 'Mary Lou'

Figure 9. Rebuslike interpretations of characters.

for syllabary learners, Worcester's chart probably fulfills any poetic functions that Sequoyah's original order once fulfilled. Many Cherokees, whether they have mastered the syllabary or not, can recite at least the first few lines of the chart. The chart is almost always read across rather than down. This means that each line rhymes with those before and after it, all the way through. A number of Cherokees I interviewed spontaneously recited the first few rows, to show how they learned or taught it. In Teacher B's Bible study and syllabary class, however, we chanted each column of the syllabary from top to bottom, producing lines that rhymed internally.

In another bit of evidence supporting the notion that the syllabary is treated as a set of syllable-long morphemes rather than as an arbitrary representation of sounds, some Cherokees involved in language education have attempted to link the shapes of individual characters with words that serve as English-language puns on their phonetic value. For example, elementary school Teacher 1 told me that she has seen others associate the character ⟨Ꮮ⟩ with the English verb "lay," because it appears to be "laying down." Exemplifying a more complicated mnemonic, another language teacher told me that she and others remembered that the character ⟨Ꮈ⟩ has the value /lu/ because, in English, ⟨Ꮈ⟩ stands for "Mary Lou" (see Figure 9).

Another practice that suggests the inherent meaningfulness of the syllabary is the means by which some speakers determine the "syl-

---

a. Spoken word: tikv:tsahltohti, 'frying pan'

b. "Spelling pronunciations" given by informant

    i. tikv:tsa<u>loh</u>tohti

      Suggested syllabary spelling = ᏝᎬᏦᎥᏬ

    ii. tikv:tsa<u>lvh</u>tohti

      Suggested syllabary spelling = ᏝᎬᎩᎥᏬ

    iii. tikv:tsa<u>lah</u>tohti

      Suggested syllabary spelling = ᏝᎬᏩᎥᏬ

c. Final choice was (iii) because of shared syllable lah with verb form tikv:tsa<u>lah</u>ka, 'he is frying.'

Figure 10. Morpho-semantic manipulations designed to produce accurate syllabary spellings.

labary" spelling of a word. As the reader understands by now, such spellings often suggest the presence of extra vowels. The problem for the writer is, which vowel to choose? In order to represent the consonant /k/, for example, the writer must choose the character /ka/, /ke/, /ki/, /ku/, /ko/, or /kv/. Some consultants told me that, when looking for the right syllable to choose, they alter the form of the word in question (change the tense, change it from a noun to a verb, and so on) until they find a form that actually contains a vowel in the appropriate space. That then tells them which syllable to choose.

An example, illustrated in Figure 10, will clarify this point. While in the field, I worked several times a week with the elderly fluent speaker considered to be the foremost authority on the *kituhwa* dialect on the Eastern Cherokee Language Project's talking dictionary. One day, in three elicitations, he gave me three different "syllabary" pronunciations for the word "frying pan." The "local" pronunciation was *tikv:tsahltohti*. The syllabary pronunciations were, first, *tikv:tsalohtohti*, then *tikv:tsalvhtohti*, and finally *tikv:tsalahtohti*. These were not intended to be variants; rather, the speaker was searching for the "right" syllabary pronunciation. (Which one is "right" is probably impossible to determine because in normal speech there is no vowel in the position in question.) When I pointed out the series of adjustments he had made, he said, "I think *lah* is most correct because of the verb form, 'he is frying': *tikʋ:tsalahka*" (see Figure 10 for the details of this interaction).

This implies that the choice of spelling is a meaningful one that provides semantic (and possibly even grammatical) information. Spelling in the syllabary is clearly not seen as merely an abstract and arbitrary means of representing the sounds of spoken language.

The Cherokee syllabary is treated with such respect and seen as such a bearer of linguistic accuracy and knowledge, then, not because, as in English, writing is seen as the *representation* of a standard of pronunciation, but rather because it is seen as *being* a standard—itself a source of semantic and historical, encoded information.

It is important to note that it is largely the *printed* syllabary as codified by Worcester in the *Phoenix* and in the New Testament that is seen as embodying this standard. Two of the consultants with whom I discussed the original Sequoyan order and his earlier, more scribal versions of the characters denied that either the earlier order or the earlier script style was truly authentic. As discussed in the last chapter, the public school Cherokee language teacher referred to the chart and print found in the New Testament by saying, "I think the original is this one." I had the following exchange with a much younger consultant, who was also literate in the syllabary:

MB: So you're saying you think [the syllabary today is] pretty much the way [Sequoyah] originally wrote it?

Consultant: Yeah, in its own entirety. The alphabet you see today, on this way, is the way that he wrote it. Exactly, I believe so.

The printed syllabary, particularly as received through the New Testament, is authentic and authenticating, an "original" system for representing the sounds of language as well as knowledge.

Local Cherokee linguistic ideologies, then, distance the syllabary from the arbitrariness of symbolic systems while reinforcing the cultural specificity of the syllabary as iconic-indexical code.

Chapter Five

What Else You Gonna Go After?

The Commodification of the Syllabary

*I*n reading the foregoing discussion of the codelike qualities of the syllabary and its perceived relationships to the spoken Cherokee language, some who have visited the Qualla Boundary only as tourists may feel skeptical. Outsiders may perceive the syllabary, in the forms in which it is presented in tourist shops, as a historical artifact or symbol of past achievements with little contemporary linguistic significance. While tourist venues like the local museum and the annual outdoor musical drama certainly celebrate the syllabary's invention and use, they may nevertheless reinforce the impression that its primary importance is historical. But this could not be further from the truth. The syllabary plays crucial roles in contemporary Cherokee life even in the most public settings. Paradoxically, it is a semiotic vehicle for boundary setting as well as for the attraction of outsiders; its iconic-indexical use enhances the value of some objects while identifying others as "not for sale."

Tourism in Cherokee

Because Cherokee is a major site of tourism in the Great Smoky Mountains, with more tourists than ever attracted by a large new casino, commodification looms large as a potential mode of transformation of objects and practices, including those related to the syllabary. Syllabary-marked commodities were to be found in most of the craft shops in downtown Cherokee in the mid-1990s, and many also carried language education materials that included syllabic writing (see Figure 11). Syllabic writing punctuates the otherwise overwhelmingly English graphic landscape of the town in patterned ways (Figures 12, 13, and 14). These patterns of distribution become more understandable in the context of some of the broader themes in Cherokee tourism.

Tourism is more than just an occasional or supplemental activity for most Eastern Cherokees. In the summer, tourism almost completely takes over and gives shape to the downtown, and to many of the surrounding Cherokee subcommunities as well, since they contain campgrounds, small grocery and supply stores, and access to rivers and hiking trails. In winters past, tourism left specters in the form of signs pointing the way to attractions, hundreds of closed businesses, and acres of empty campgrounds. It is not as though tourism can be separated out from the "normal" life of the place. Rather, it represents one of the poles of the seasonal cycle that has been normal life in this community for the past few generations. These days, a new rhythm has emerged, with more businesses staying open year-round to accommodate visitors to the casino that opened in 1996.

Many Eastern Cherokees living on the Boundary while I was there made a seasonal living or supplemented another income during the summer months through the tourist industry. However, many of the tourist-oriented businesses on the Boundary were owned by non-Indians.

According to the 1990 U.S. census, which contained the most up-to-date demographic data on the community available at the time of my fieldwork, unemployment was relatively high and part-time employment was the norm. Overall, approximately 18 percent of the civilian labor force was unemployed, with 14 percent unemployment among women and 21 percent among men (U.S. Bureau of the Census 1990b: 1063, Table 225). Roughly 37 percent of adult male workers were employed full-time, while for women the comparable figure was 30 percent (U.S. Bureau of the Census 1990b: 1066, Table 228).

The per capita income in this community for 1989 was $6,382. The median household income was $16,330. The median income of men working full-time in 1989 was $14,854, compared to $9,118 for seasonal

CHEROKEE WORDS
ᏣᎳᎩ ᏗᎦᏁᎢᏍᏗ
tsa la gi   di ka ne i s di

acorn	ᎫᎴ gu le	
Amen	ᎡᎺᏅ e me nv	
and	ᎠᎴ a le	
anvil	ᎠᏐᏗ ᏔᎷᎩᏍᎩ ᎤᎵᎩ a so di ta lu gi s gi u li gi	
apple	ᏒᎦᏔ sv ga ta	
apron	ᎠᏤᏌᏙ a tse sa do	
arrow	ᏗᎦᏓᏝᏛ di ga da tla dv	
arrow-heads	ᏗᎦᏓᏝᏛ ᏧᏍᎪ di ga da tla dv tsu s go	
ashes	ᎪᏍᏚ go s du	
aunt	ᎡᏠᎩ e tlo gi	
ax	ᎦᎷᏯᏍᏗ ga lu ya s di	
baby	ᎤᏍᏗᎦ u s di ga	
bad	ᎤᏲᎢ u yo i	
bag	ᏕᎦᎶᏗ de ga lo di	
ball	ᎠᎳᏍᎦᎶᏗ a la s ga lo di	
barrel	ᏒᏙᏂ sv do ni	
basket	ᏔᎷᏣ ta lu tsa	
bass (fish)	ᎤᏃᎦ u no ga	

Figure 11. Page from *Cherokee Words with Pictures,* by Mary Ulmer Chiltoskey, p. 5. Copyright 1972 by Mary Ulmer and G. B. Chiltoskey. (Courtesy of Cherokee Publications, Cherokee, N.C.)

Figure 12. Frankoma pottery trivet with syllabary design. (Photograph by Lisa J. Lefler)

male workers. Women who worked full-time and year-round had a median income of $12,240, compared to $5,956 for less than full-time workers (U.S. Bureau of the Census 1990b: 1066, Table 228). Approximately 35 percent of all persons for whom poverty status was determined had income below poverty level in 1989 (U.S. Bureau of the Census 1990b: 67, Table 16).

The most visible source of employment on the reserve is certainly the tourism industry, but the census figures suggest that the most common full-time occupations for employed Eastern Cherokees in 1990 were actually in some level of civil service, with government workers accounting for approximately 38 percent of employed Native American adults. Another 22 percent were reported to be in professional occupations, such as health care or education, with another 22 percent in manufacturing (U.S. Bureau of the Census 1990b: 66, Table 15). Construction accounted for 14 percent of jobs, and retail trade 10 percent (U.S. Bureau of the Census 1990b: 1062, Table 224). However, considering that most Cherokees derived their income from part-time and

Figure 13. Sign on the door of Cherokee Elementary School in downtown Cherokee. The syllabary portion reads *Tsalaki Tsunsti?i Tsunatohlekwasti?i*, 'Cherokee Elementary School.' (Photograph by Lisa J. Lefler)

seasonal work, rather than full-time, year-round jobs, the local importance of the tourism industry is clearly underrepresented in these numbers.

Tourism and "traditionalism" can complement each other; quite a few Cherokees were primarily engaged in "traditional occupations," at least as of the 1980 census. At that time, there were four dancers, one drummer or singer, one potter, twenty basket makers, six beaders, eight carvers, two fan makers, four moccasin makers, six quilters, and fifteen others engaged in handworking occupations (Reddy 1993: 650, 652). Certainly, many more Cherokees did this kind of work on a part-time basis.

With its low per capita income levels, high unemployment, and underemployment, the community clearly has needed tourism for its survival. But tourism always entails intrusions, impositions, and disruptions. And in the case of cultural tourism, visitors actively seek

Figure 14. Sign for a clinic in downtown Cherokee. (Photograph by Lisa J. Lefler)

to appropriate cultural objects or at least to immerse themselves in local cultural experiences, usually without the background needed to do so appropriately or with sensitivity. Many Eastern Cherokees therefore see tourism as a sort of inescapable burden, the harmful effects of which they seek to minimize.

Commodification and Value

The types of institutions catering to tourists, in addition to the casino, include motels, restaurants, gift shops, produce stands, businesses that display captive bears, campgrounds, amusement centers, two bingo halls, a wax museum (closed in 1995), a chairlift, a living village, an outdoor historical drama, an educational museum, fish hatcheries, and an artists' cooperative. Some of these establishments benefit the tribe directly; in other cases the profits go to individuals.

In this context, where entertainment is purchased, and where purchasing is posited as a form of entertainment, much of what *can* be commodified *is* commodified. In a practice known as "chiefing," Cherokee men dressed in Plains Indian garb receive tips from tourists for providing an "Indian" presence—and particularly for having their picture taken.[1] What is being commodified in this case is authentic Indianness, it being irrelevant that what tourists see as authentically Indian (a Plains Indian) is not authentically Cherokee.

In the earlier discussions of the syllabary as code, I argued that reading and writing, script and printing, are differently valued as elements within an overall system of Cherokee language practices. This is value in a Saussurean sense—a set of meanings that can only be understood as a total system, mutually limiting and defining (de Saussure 1959: 111–22). We saw, for example, that while reading printed Cherokee aloud generally has value as a Christian practice, writing Cherokee script idiosyncratically does not. In fact, the latter may raise suspicion of witchcraft. These values are structural; they become more or less relevant in particular contexts of usage but are generally shared across a wide spectrum of the community.

In the arena of commodification, the syllabary acquires value in the Marxian sense. This concerns the sense in which language use of various types is productive: creating events or artifacts. Marxian value is "the transformation of the dynamic content of productive activity into the category of meaning through which it is oriented, represented and coordinated as a part of a total system of production" (Turner 1984: 7). This type of value can be differentially distributed in a society, for example via unequal access to types of language use such as writing.

Also relevant here are the Marxian subcategories of use-value and exchange-value (Marx 1977: 125–77). Although these categories will become somewhat problematized in the course of my discussion, they are useful starting points for talking about the syllabary's semiotic value in the context of tourism. Use-value refers to the functions a commodity may serve due to its particular qualities—being a mug, say, or a T-shirt, or a performance that can be viewed (and hence, consumed on the spot). Exchange-value will refer in this context to the ability of a commodity to be bought and sold.

In the tourist arena in general, use-value is nearly eclipsed by exchange-value as the dominant mode in which to produce and categorize practices and objects. This can be seen fairly clearly in Cherokee basket-making. Cherokee split oak and rivercane baskets are famous and extremely labor-intensive. The price for a functional basket, though usually quite a bargain in light of the labor-power involved, is often more than the average tourist is willing to pay. As a result, some Cherokee basket makers produce nonfunctional miniatures, and even tiny baskets that are turned into earrings.

As we will see, questions quickly arise as to how to define "use" where syllabary-marked commodities are concerned. When an object is marked with syllabary, it sometimes has multiple potential use-values. The object itself may be functional, as a trivet, for example (see Figure 12), and then the text on it may be functional in the sense that it conveys meaning. This latter semiotic use-value may be broken down into the three categories we have been considering throughout—the iconic, the indexical, and the symbolic. When the syllabary text has the most symbolic use-value, that is, where it is most likely to be used as a system for recording or producing spoken language, or to convey specific semantic content, it is likely to have left the world of commodities altogether. In other words, it is likely in those circumstances to have the least use-value as a nonlinguistic object.

The iconic-indexical value foregrounding the Cherokee cultural specificity of practices and objects is prominent in tourism as it is in other aspects of Cherokee life. This value characterizes a place, an experience, or the creator of an artifact as specifically and uniquely Cherokee and characterizes the consumer/reader as being Cherokee or as having been in Cherokee, North Carolina. In Cherokee, where making contact with one's "roots" is such an important part of the experience for so many tourists, items and experiences may have special appeal if they can be used by tourists to assert their own claims of Cherokee identity. Objects may be marked in such a way as to acquire this value whether their history of production lends them that value or not. For example, a local manufacturing company that makes pan-Indian knickknacks for sale on the Boundary and nationwide is called "The Cherokees." A sign on the building boasts, "The Largest Group of Indian Craftsmen in the U.S." Through labeling, these *non*-culturally specific Indian artifacts become "Cherokee."[2]

The Cherokee gift shops, among which there was a striking sameness of proffered merchandise in the mid-1990s, generally carried bric-a-brac, toys, and clothing, with Cherokee, pan-Indian, Appalachian, or pan-Southern themes. Examples of each type would include, respectively, Cherokee baskets, toy feather headdresses and plastic tomahawks, "hillbilly" gag gifts, and Confederate flags.

The syllabary was an important marker of Cherokee cultural specificity in these commodities. Commodities identifiable as Cherokee quite frequently had something to do with Sequoyah or with the syllabary. Of the fifty-two craft shops I visited in downtown Cherokee, thirty carried at least one type of object with syllabary somewhere on it.

Commodification is a great equalizer. As Marx said, the exchange-value of commodities obscures the social relations that underlie their production and consumption (Marx 1977: 163–77). In the tourism context, use-value and the social value of objects nearly disappear in the shadow of genericism and exchange-value. The sharp differentiation among types of indexical value carried by the syllabary—its ability to point to different types of users, texts, and contexts by way of differences in form—also seems largely collapsed in this context. This is because the differential distribution of syllabary usage, cultural presuppositions concerning the special revelatory nature of the syllabary, concerns about its relationship to the spoken language, and so on are largely invisible and possibly irrelevant to the outsider. Print versus handwriting, reading versus writing—such distinctions are beyond the discernment of the tourist in search of consumable artifacts and experiences.

Even in those specialized contexts within the tourist industry, such as the museums and the drama, that *do* emphasize the cultural specificity of the syllabary, that emphasis goes hand in hand with additional emphases on the historical—that is, past—glory of the syllabary, and on the syllabary's role in supporting the Cherokees on the road to a generic, non–culturally specific type of civilization. Sequoyah and the syllabary are Cherokee, but their function in this context is inclusive, not exclusive—homogenizing, not differentiating. As the Janus-faced mugs with a Plains-headdress-adorned figure on one side and the syllabary on the other collapse distinctions between Cherokees and other Indians, so tourist offerings like *Unto These Hills* collapse distinctions between Cherokees and other civilized Americans.

Comparison with Volkman's (1990) study of Toraja tourism suggests two additional ways in which commodification erases distinctions. Volkman identifies a collapsing of time that occurs in the process of commodification that, in this case, seems to justify the consumption of the syllabary. The person of Sequoyah and the historical moment of the chart are made timeless and offered alongside a kind of naturalized present. Sequoyah and the syllabary become "essences," rather than a historical figure and the tool he invented, and so can be much more easily digested. Volkman also suggests that the mass reproduction of a particular cultural image can generate a kind of fixity, as it does with the appearance of the syllabary in general and with the chart in particular. This fixity has made of the syllabary a kind of logo of Cherokee ethnicity and heritage.

In cultural tourism, the commodified experiences and objects are designed to entertain and educate at the same time. Tourists want to leave their vacation spot with a sense of having had a cross-cultural experience, being able to say that they have learned something. Yet, being on vacation, they are generally not in search of fundamental challenge or discomfort.

The syllabary's iconic-indexical capacities lend it perfectly to this scheme. It has the *appearance* of representing knowledge. What I mean by this is that it is arranged in one of the ways significant information is arranged in other linguistic and cultural traditions—in a chart or a tablet. Fogelson has pointed out that Sequoyah's pose with the scroll— or occasionally, as in the now defunct Cherokee wax museum, with a tablet—is highly reminiscent of Moses with the Ten Commandments (Raymond D. Fogelson, pers. com., 1994). And yet the tourist does not need to take it too seriously. He or she receives the cue to this effect from the placement of the syllabary chart in places where other non-denotational, decorative signs are placed—on key rings, mugs, and so on. Those stores that sell Cherokee language books are likely to have them placed alongside cookbooks, joke books, and so on.

The juncture of entertainment and education can be seen outside the tourist context as well when nonspeakers are brought in contact with the syllabary. Unlike fluent native speakers, who frequently learn the syllabary through Bible study and on their own, nonspeakers in Cherokee language classes are more likely to be exposed to puzzles, fill-in-the-blank exercises, and so on. In one adult language class, a teacher proposed that the all non-Indian class's work toward learning the syllabary be transformed into a group project that would produce a children's coloring book. The idea was to have fun, to learn the syllabary (that is, to be able to produce pages that combined syllabic and phonetic spellings with illustrations), and to produce a commodity for sale. Teacher and students were quite enthusiastic about this project and saw it as a logical extension of the syllabary's uses in the classroom, although to the best of my knowledge the project was not completed.

Sameness, Difference, and Accessibility

In the mid-1990s, many Cherokee community members wanted to communicate to outside visitors in general, and to tourists in particu-lar, that "our lives are just like yours" or that "we are just like you." I heard frustration with tourists' lack of understanding of this point from shop owners, both white and Cherokee, and from other Chero-kees who had a good deal of contact with outsiders. One young adult Cherokee told me, "See, I've had people before ask me if I still lived in a log home, you know, didn't have electricity or nothing and I'd just have to tell 'em that my life is no different, my lifestyle is no different than yours." This point of view was even reflected in the speech delivered by the tour guide at Cherokee's living Indian village. Despite the unfamiliar appearance of the recreated eighteenth-century village, its housing, the crafts being produced, and the clothing being worn by the village's make-believe residents, the tour guide reassured visitors that contemporary residents of Cherokee live no differently than they do.

But sameness cannot be the central or only message of successful cultural tourism. This kind of tourism requires the commodification of culture—as education, entertainment, and, more generally, experience, and in the form of objects for sale. In order to be desirable to the consumer, these commodities must be such that the visitor could not obtain them in his or her everyday life. The visitor uses the commodities later—via pictures shown, stories told, or objects demonstrated—as indexes of having been to this particular place and no other. Visitors to Cherokee may also use such commodities to indexically mark themselves as pilgrims who have made their trip in order to reestablish a connection with their "roots" or "heritage."

There is a tension, then, between the desire of residents of this community to disabuse tourists of stereotyped misconceptions about Indian life, and their need to offer experiences and commodities that are unique and even exotic.

This tension is echoed by another, related dilemma of self-representation in Cherokee tourism—and history, too, for that matter. The dilemma is whether to stress the Cherokees' history as foremost among the "civilized tribes," an emphasis that might assist in the goal of convincing tourists that Cherokees are "just like themselves," or to stress the ways in which Cherokee culture and history diverge from the culture and history of white America. The latter approach supports the exoticizing of the syllabary, and in the mid-1990s it was pursued either via the pan-Indianizing of Cherokee culture or by way of its naturalization.[3] Paradoxically, Cherokee "civilization" may be seen as exotic at the same time as it is familiar to the tourist because of its "otherness" as a feature of Indian, rather than Euro-American, culture.

The syllabary itself proves to be an exemplary site for working out these tensions: it is simultaneously representative of a status marker shared with white American civilization *and* something unique and foreign-looking to outsiders. But what is it that makes this writing unique and foreign? There is a story about a Westerner who, upon first arriving in an East Asian city, was enchanted and intrigued by the foreign and, he expected, exotic written messages that plastered the city streets. He was disenchanted later, however, upon learning that the signs that had so captured his imagination communicated meanings like "laundry" and "fresh fish." Writing appears exotic, that is, linked in an exclusive way with a culturally specific other, only when it is not understood. By this I do not mean only that the specific content of signs or pages is not understood—in other words that the viewer is illiterate in and may not even speak the language in question. The ultimate exoticism of writing is achieved if the viewer does not even understand in general terms *how* the system is related to spoken language. In all likelihood this means that the system is unrelated to his or her own. But the strangeness is heightened by the fact that she or he does not know how the system works—is it phonetic, logographic, ideographic, pictographic? Writing may seem most exotic of all if it is not even clear that it *is* writing, if the viewer does not even fully understand its *capacity* to be related to spoken language or, perhaps, the capacity of the symbols to be reproduced by an individual human writer. Writing is most exotic, then, when it just barely works for the viewer as an icon of meaningful writing.

In spite of the syllabary's location at the pinnacle of the Cherokees' civilized achievements, many of the ways in which it was used in tourism in the mid-1990s sought to capture its potential exoticism. That is, it was used in ways writing is not generally used, as in the creation of nonlinguistic designs, and was thereby distanced from its identity as writing. Many of the items designed with syllabary, such as blackened pottery, otherwise featured geometric or pictographic designs. Syllabary used in these contexts almost never had specific referential (symbolic) meaning.

In order to deemphasize the syllabary's exoticism, it would be necessary to show how, or at least that, it works as a referential system and specifically as a system for representing spoken language. There were also products that served this purpose in the tourist arena—language books and certain single-page printed texts, usually hymns and prayers containing syllabary, phonetics, and translation. The syllabary was demystified in such products. Its potential to convey meaning was evidenced by the translation, and its representational mechanics were revealed through the phonetic spellings provided alongside the syllabary characters.

Some products, then, emphasized the exoticism of the syllabary while others sought to demystify it for tourists, to reassure them that the syllabary is a functioning writing system with equivalence to their own. However, the functions of the two types of products overlapped. Buried in each type were hints at the other. Objects that foregrounded the syllabary as icon and index often included embedded information about its potential as a symbolic orthography; texts that unveiled its orthographic mechanics also frequently presented an exotic "look" or carried exoticizing associations. Both the Sequoyah Cafeteria sign and the syllabary-marked pottery, while appearing to be randomly designed to the outsider, meticulously preserved the original Sequoyan order of the syllabary. This is the order in which Sequoyah always reproduced the syllabary, and in which it was reproduced by monolingual Cherokees, for whom the chart has little value, well into this century. Alternatively, the syllabary markings on other pieces of pottery replicated conventional chart order. There was thus nothing random about the decorative use of syllabary in these contexts, and the order of the syllabary characters on them furthermore pointed toward a history of meaningful orthographic use.

Nor were the knickknacks marked with syllabary randomly marked. Rather, they were designed with the ubiquitous syllabary chart, a chart that not only contains phonetic equivalents for the characters but also dates back to the origins of Cherokee printing, newspaper publishing, constitution writing, and Christian conversion. This chart, with which the reader is already familiar, was introduced to the Cherokee reading public by Samuel Worcester in the first issue of the *Cherokee Phoenix* in 1828 (see Figure 1). The chart arranged the characters alphabetically and gave phonetic spellings, both clearly useful only to those who already read English. The chart thus hearkens back to a primal codification at the time at which the Cherokees were "civilized" like other literate Americans. This history, these meanings, were implied in these commodities, even if the chart was too small to be properly read. In other words, even when the syllabary was clearly being used as a design, in contexts and on surfaces where designs were otherwise located, and when the syllabary's predictable relationship with spoken language was obscured, its systematicity, which could ultimately rest only on its link to spoken language, was preserved.

Similarly, the commodities that made explicit the syllabary's link with spoken language, and therefore its being "just like" the English alphabet, contained hints of exoticism. These hints generally took the form of naturalization, pan-Indianization, or temporal displacement, which functioned as a secondary type of naturalization. I elaborate on these three vehicles of exoticization below.

At both the annual Fall Festival and at "Kituwah," an annual pow-wow in Asheville, North Carolina, in which many Eastern Cherokees participate, booths run by Cherokee language teachers have offered the writing of consumers' names in Cherokee (in the syllabary) for sale.[4] The purpose of these booths was to raise funds, via the sale of commodities, for one or more programs in the tribal school system.

The first time I saw such a booth, at "Kituwah" in September 1992, a language teacher was offering "your name written in Cherokee" for two dollars. Most of the customers seemed to be children. A sign also offered the option to "ask questions about the Cherokee language." Syllabary calendars were also offered for sale. A natural-looking cloth or skin, bearing a syllabary chart, was draped across the table. On top of the table rested the Cherokee New Testament, the hymnal, a Cherokee dictionary, and a laminated copy of the front page of the *Cherokee Phoenix* from 1828. Hanging from the front of the table was a cloth map of the Qualla Boundary, with the various Eastern Cherokee community names written in syllabary. The context of this powwow, which attracts many non-Indian tourists as well as Indian artists and performers from around the country, provides the opportunity for a blending of the historical and the contemporary (the *Phoenix* alongside the contemporary community map) as well as the sacred (the New Testament) and the profane (the production and sale of commodities). In this context, there is no need for a rigid distinction between the types of syllabary usage that generally characterize the homes of literate speakers on the one hand and the downtown tourist shops on the other.

A booth at the Cherokee Fall Festival in 1993, described earlier, also offered the writing of names in syllabary for sale, in a slightly different context. This booth, run by another language teacher with the assistance of students, was raising funds for a particular class at the high school. Along with the names, which were written on small pieces of wood, the booth offered candy bars and raffle tickets for a "lightning" design, finger-woven belt. The syllabary names might be seen as an intermediate type of commodity between the immediately consumable (the candy bar) and the good-luck charm (the raffle ticket). Part of what one was purchasing was the immediate pleasure of seeing one's name transformed into a possibly foreign, or at least extraordinary, script. The other part was having a little piece of syllabary, on a "natural" substance, to carry around. This booth also sold T-shirts bearing syllabic and phonetic writing of Cherokee along with English.

The most popular Cherokee language book for sale in the downtown Cherokee shops in the mid-1990s, *Cherokee Words with Pictures* (Chiltoskey 1972) by Mary Chiltoskey, contains English and then Cherokee words, written in both syllabary and phonetics. Many of the pictures that accompany selected words represent plants and animals; others selectively illustrate words that refer to pan-Indian cultural objects—arrows, teepees, tomahawks, and a "girl" with a feather rising from the back of her headband. The *Cherokee A-B-C Coloring Book with Words in English and Cherokee* (Pennington and Bushyhead 1994), a children's book that features syllabary, narrates its pictures of Cherokee life exclusively in the past tense and depicts a prehistoric way of life—Cherokees in loincloths wielding arrows and flint knives. One page (unnumbered) notes, "The Cherokee traveled through the forest on trails. Sometimes the trails were made by the animals." A Cherokee acquaintance who planned to produce her own syllabary coloring book intended to have the pages feature the indigenous plants and animals of the Cherokees' native Smoky Mountains.

One of the larger available versions of the syllabary chart was on a colorful six-inch by nine-inch postcard. At the top, the postcard bore the title "Cherokee Alphabet" (note that is does not say "syllabary"), inviting the tourist to compare this writing system to the one he or she probably uses every day. And indeed, underneath this heading was the chart, as arranged by Samuel Worcester, but handwritten. However, surrounding the chart were pictographic symbols of uncertain origin, with nothing indicating to the tourist that these symbols are not *also* part of the "Cherokee alphabet."

Single-page reprints of hymns and prayers in syllabary were printed on mock parchment, suggesting antiquity or temporal distance at the same time that the Cherokees' Christian sameness was being affirmed.

The complex relationship between the functional, and therefore recognizable, usage of the syllabary as an orthography and its use as a design or icon-index of Indianness was mirrored in the distribution of syllabary in the general graphic landscape of Cherokee, North Carolina. Syllabary signs have a lot of semiotic work to do because they mark a geographic space inhabited by two superimposed cultural landscapes. On the one hand, there is the flashy, public downtown Cherokee known to tourists, with its shops, attractions, and neon. On the other, there is the functional infrastructure of the Cherokee community. The important tribal offices, community centers, and schools are somewhat off the beaten tourist path, set back from the roads.

These two dimensions of downtown correspond very roughly to two main north-south roads, which begin and end at nearly exactly the same points but one of which functions as the tourists' road and one of which tends to handle more local traffic. The first takes motorists past shops, restaurants, and gas stations, one after the other, and often moves very slowly on weekends. Tourists basically stick to this and a few other main roads in Cherokee. The mountains inhabited by much of the rest of the community, and hence the everyday, contemporary life of most Cherokees, are invisible to outsiders. The other main north-south road accesses the tribal housing office, high school, fire station, manufacturing businesses, and private homes. It is in the latter places, and particularly in signs marking the entrances to many of these buildings, that a visitor would see the syllabary in use as a symbolic orthography used to form words that have the capacity to communicate semantic content. This, in addition to the types of content—generally, the identities of modern, bureaucratic institutions—would well serve the goal of communicating the cultural sameness discussed above. What better evidence could there be that Cherokees, even down to the usage of their writing system in everyday life, are just like the visitor? But ironically, these are parts of the reservation that are less visible to the outside visitor, and unlike the Sequoyah Cafeteria sign, these signs generally cannot be seen from the road. However, if a tourist does stumble onto one of these signs, it surely presents a case for the functionality of the syllabary, and at the same time suggests to the visitor that this is a bilingual, biscriptal, community, different in a significant way from his or her own.

Both of these apparent sets of syllabary usage, in the tourists' downtown and in the Cherokee bureaucratic downtown, are to some extent superficial, meaning that they do not fully represent actual usage of the syllabary in daily Cherokee life. That is, the syllabary is not used *primarily* as a design or treated as decorative, and it is probably *never* considered to be pan-Indian, in the everyday lives of those who are literate in it. Nor is it likely that people who read syllabary use the syllabary signs marking bureaucratic institutions to find or identify those institutions, although it seems clear that they are sources of local pride. Primary usage of the syllabary as an orthography takes place elsewhere, outside the realm of tourism—in churches, classrooms, and possibly still in some usage of medicinal manuscripts.

There are three layers of visibility, then, in terms of the syllabary's presence in Cherokee's graphic landscape: (1) the most visible syllabary, occurring in and corresponding to the showy tourist-oriented main streets of downtown; (2) the apparently functional syllabary marking the community's bureaucratic infrastructure, where tourists may happen upon it; and, finally, (3) the presence, most functional in terms of communication of semantic content but invisible to the outsider, of the syllabary in the actual residential community of Cherokee.

This layered semiotic landscape, with varying degrees of opacity, provides a kind of protection from the outsiders on whom a community like Cherokee largely depends. Without the existence and easy accessibility of the second layer, the bureaucratic downtown, with its glimpse into a more normal and yet culturally distinct way of life and its unadvertised syllabary signs, the tourist might look further for the "real" Cherokee. But perhaps seeing Cherokees going about their daily business on these secondary roads and noting that, for instance, the syllabary is put to more practical use as a writing system here than it generally is in the tourist shops, the visitor may feel he has found it—the home town of, as John Finger described them, the "Cherokee Americans" (Finger 1991). But there is little chance that, via signs or commodities, the code will provide tourists with access to the kinds of protected, culturally specific knowledge discussed in Chapter 3. Lacking the proper background, outsiders will never be able to get at the code's underlying meanings. Since the "code" only becomes fully transparent when the right intentionality is combined with the right context (e.g., Bible reading on the part of someone "saved"), there is little danger of the code being broken by those in the wrong context with the wrong intentionality.

The Limits of Commodification

It was not uncommon for language teachers to step from their teaching role into a commodity-producing mode. It was considered acceptable to market one's real knowledge of the Cherokee language in order to become a language teacher or even to produce commodities of the type discussed above. As in the case of the booths selling one's "name in Cherokee," such commodification is especially acceptable if it is not for *personal* profit but for community fund-raising. A number of language teachers also turned their knowledge and abilities toward the production of commercial language education materials. Four former or current language teachers were or were planning to be involved in the production of some type of dictionary. A few had produced language tapes. The Eastern Cherokee Language Project (discussed in Chapter 4) was primarily set up to produce texts and other materials with a heavy concentration of educational use-value. Videotapes of elders conversing and performing traditional activities like cooking bean bread, picking greens, and so on, the videotaped and written language lessons, and the talking dictionary were all products meant to be used, and specifically to be used by the tribal school system. But these products also had an exchange-value. Who had the rights to this value may yet be an undecided matter. But there was no evident dispute as to the propriety of producing commodities of this sort.

Neither selling the use of one's knowledge and fluency nor using these to produce commodities for sale was seen as a problem in itself. Therefore, the buying of language education materials was seen as a benign activity, whether engaged in by non-Indians or local Cherokees. But the purchase of knowledge and fluency *itself* was cast as a threat and a real problem. One of my consultants, a former language teacher of both children and adults and a social service worker at the time of our interview, was very concerned about this. This was her response when I asked what motivated her adult students, a mix of Cherokees and non-Cherokees, to take her Cherokee language class.

> Well, I was hoping it was good purpose—well, for learning so we won't lose our language, you know. But later on, I found—it wasn't none of my students, but I found some people that learned from the other person, they were learning how to talk so they can get enrolled in Cherokee, . . . saying that they could talk Indian. And what they were doing was learning from those Indian words so they can take it up to Cherokee, and go to the office, saying my great-grandmother talked Indian, and this the way she talked, . . . and I thought that was dishonest, and I didn't feel right about that. I mean, that didn't make me feel good about it. If you want to learn Cherokee language, don't use it like that, you know.

I started to ask whether the scheme she was describing was even workable. Was it really possible that someone's ability to speak Cherokee could affect his or her tribal enrollment status?

> I guess it worked for them. They said they put lot of—lot of 'em in the roll. And I can't prove it, but I have heard a lot of people said they got enrolled, and right now [a] man works and—he's calling himself a chief, and . . . I was told he doesn't even look like Indian at all. He's a redneck. And saying he's a chief, that he can get you—give you a green card where you can be enrolled in Cherokee, North Carolina.
>
> If you'd learn Indian language just to get in the roll, that's not right. That's cheating—that's cheating more of Indian people again! And I feel like we was treated bad enough as it was, without—If you are Indian people, you ought to be able to prove it yourself, and you ought to be able to do that on your own, without learning Indian language.

Her anger over this scenario was reflective of a more general resentment in the community toward those who, in search of the supposed plethora of benefits available to Native Americans, acquired tribal enrollment status to which they are not truly entitled from the local point of view. Being Cherokee is not considered an acquired status, nor does Cherokee identity have exchange-value. You cannot *learn* to be Cherokee; you just have to *be* it. Her insistence on this point, and the plausibility of her story about (non-Indian) students taking Cherokee language classes in order to bolster their claim of being Cherokee, may in part reflect the widely held belief that Cherokee is the identity most often claimed by Indian "wannabees."[5]

The affronts she recounted became deeper and deeper, more and more personal, as she moved from language to enrollment to her people's bones themselves. "Yeah," she said, indignantly, "to use what Indians—what little Indians still got left. Just like, we went to demonstrate [against] grave-diggers. They going in the grave, and take these bone[s] out, and sell it for Halloween, for something like that. And I told 'em, why do you go back in our Indian grave and still get money off the bone? You put 'em there, and took everything away from us, now you want our bone. If we run outta bones, what else you gonna go after?" Being Cherokee, and being a native speaker of Cherokee—these are things that cannot be bought, they can only be stolen. Those who would try to do so are no better than grave-robbers.

This may be part of the reason why it is so important to authenticate one's cultural knowledge with knowledge and appropriate usage of the syllabary. Outsiders can learn the syllabary's phonetic values from a syllabary chart or language book, but they will not learn the secret of ⟨R⟩ and ⟨R⟩, the dropping of the last syllable in a hymn, the Book of John.

Fear of cultural robbery is generated not just by greedy individual outsiders; it is also considered possible that other Indian groups might try to claim what is distinctively Cherokee. A Cherokee educator told me that an elder was approached and offered a sum of money by representatives of another tribe. According to the story, this other tribe wanted to use the elder's knowledge of the Cherokee language to provide evidence that they themselves had a native language, evidence that might be used to support a plea for federal recognition.[6]

Clearly, some things—most basically, the qualities of really being Cherokee and really speaking Cherokee—are simply not accepted as commodifiable. Although these qualities may provide individuals with the right or opportunity to produce and sell specific practices and artifacts, these qualities themselves cannot be purchased by outsiders.

That there are limits to what is seen as appropriate commodification of culture generally, and of the syllabary in particular, is well borne out by my field experience. In one downtown tourist shop, I noticed a gravestone on which the writing was all in syllabary. This gravestone was among a collection of artifacts that were on display in one section of the store. It was not for sale. Nevertheless, most Cherokees I talked to seemed to feel that a gift shop was not an appropriate place for such an object.

Generally speaking, although many shops carried an eye-catching and user-friendly book of Cherokee psalms sung as hymns in syllabary and phonetics, few sold the two syllabary items Cherokees are more likely to have in their homes than any others. The Cherokee New Testament, of which both hard cover and paperback versions are available, and the pocket-sized, inexpensive book of Cherokee hymns that many older Cherokee women carry around in their purses were for the most part absent from store shelves. It seems unlikely that this is only because these books contain no English; tourists purchased mugs and key chains bearing only the syllabary chart, a collection of written symbols with no semantic attachments whatsoever, for their iconic-indexical value. It seems plausible to assume that they might do the same with an actual (that is, symbolically meaningful, though not to them) text.

It is clear that there are important differences in the indexical capacities of syllabary texts. Some are extremely crucial markers of Cherokee identity and linguistic fluency (the Testament and hymnal); others are staples of the gift shops. Although it did not seem particularly to matter whether such objects as the New Testament were *present* in the tourism context (possibly to lend authority and depth to the salesperson's expertise), these serious, religious objects were generally withheld from the world of cultural commodities.

Just as syllabary became more and more orthographically "useful" as it moved away from the downtown and out of sight of tourists, so the orthographic use-value of a syllabary object from the Cherokee point of view is *inversely* proportional to its exchangeability.

Most of my consultants also considered it extremely inappropriate to sell, or to profit financially from, knowledge of what is considered to be traditional Cherokee medicinal and spiritual practice. The relationship between Cherokee medicine and the Cherokee language is a strong one, with sacred curing texts having been recorded in the syllabary since the time of Sequoyah's invention. This attitude toward the sale of medicinal knowledge and practice was not new, according to one consultant whose father was a medicine man. He believed that taking money for treatments robbed them of their potency. "Some of 'em would want to give money, you know, to pay him. He didn't want that. He said money was too heavy. He would rather take food, you know."

While payment was an inappropriate mode of exchange between client and doctor, providing food was appropriate. Money, on the other hand, was too "heavy." She said, "It was just like selling what you knew, and then he said after a while it wouldn't be worth anything, you know, the medicines. . . . Like it would be just weeds, you know, or roots, or something, and it wouldn't do anything for you."

Selling what you know, then, has negative consequences. "Weeds" or "roots" were all that was left of the medicine when the formula and ritual (the specialized knowledge of the medicine man) were removed or made powerless.

Occasionally, patients were insistent about paying with money. "Some of 'em [would] say, well, here take it, I'm giving you this. And he would say, just lay it down. Mama had to get it. . . . They would just put it down, and after they [left], he would say, Mary, there's some money there. And she would get it, then hand it to him, and that way, you know, it was all right. But yet, he would rather take food. . . . They would say well, go down to supermarket, I'll have a bag of flour, or bag of coffee, you know, or I'll have some food down there waiting for you." Money could be exchanged, then, but the exchange had to be mediated by a third party, and even that intermediary was not handed the money directly.

The medicine man's wife, the mediating party, was the one normally responsible for providing food. Her intervention thus possibly constituted a semiotic mediation, a transformation of too-heavy cash into an acceptable consumable form. Note that the exchange had to be of use-value for use-value; the medicine man did not have a "rate" and there was no measure of equivalency. So even the *possibility* of commodification, which requires the establishment of exchange-value, was thwarted in this context.

She went on to confirm that her father never bought or sold written

copies of medicine. Her mother, however, although she did not practice the traditional medicine to the same extent that her father did,
sought to profit from the knowledge contained in his notebooks after
his death. This consultant clearly disapproved of her mother's behavior and indicated that it had backfired. I asked her what had finally
happened to the notebooks.

> I don't know what she really done with 'em. She says that her
> house was broken into, but I don't really think so. And she says
> that she had somebody check it out, to see who got the books,
> and it pointed toward [a particular Cherokee community], and—
> she said I know who got 'em. But—the person that she names
> out, doesn't know nothing about Indian. He's an Indian, but he
> used to come up to Daddy and he'd be doctored. He was—he
> believed in Indian medicine, and Indian remedies, and all that,
> but he didn't even . . . talk in Indian. . . . He's always talked
> English . . . but she says that he's the one that got 'em. That this
> man that looked it up told him that that's where they are—the
> books are. But I know that, for a fact, she give those books, or
> she let this man—white man—borrow these books, and he went
> to make copies of 'em. He didn't know nothing about Indian; he
> just knew . . . what Indians could do, and that was gonna be his
> example, of what they can put on paper, how they put their reme-
> dies . . . medicines on the paper, that they could write it down as
> well as English. And so he went to make copies of the pages on
> that book, . . . but he brought it back and he paid her, and that's
> what she was after, was the money. . . . I had told Mom, I said,
> don't be showing everybody the books. But I think that what hap-
> pened was that she must have loaned it out, and it didn't come
> back . . . or she—she forgets. She's forgot a lot of things, and then
> you tell her, or you ask her about it, or so on, she'll say, well, so
> and so got it. But I don't know that they did.

Her mother lost track of the notebooks and asked someone to use
divination to locate them. When the divining method (unidentified)
"pointed toward" a particular community on the reservation, she concluded that a specific person had the books, possibly due to prior hos-
tility between them. My consultant's theory was that the books were

lost when her mother lent them *in exchange for money* to a white re-searcher, who never returned them. So the practice of "renting" these particular syllabic texts went beyond resulting in their losing power; in what might be seen as a stronger supernatural sanction, the texts themselves were lost.

I had an extremely moving experience while in Cherokee that fur-ther illustrates the limits of syllabic commodification. I noted earlier that the syllabary tends not to be used as a medium of individual cre-ativity. I encountered a most intriguing counterexample, however, late in my stay in Cherokee. Adult Cherokee language Teacher A showed me an original poem she had written in the syllabary, accompanied by a small drawing. She showed this to me during the course of a taped interview, asking me to read the poem aloud. She seemed pleased to have the opportunity both to test my shaky reading skills and to have someone else read her poem out loud and record it. However, despite the larger context in which nearly everything was potentially commodifiable, and despite the fact that the beauty of her sketch and almost calligraphic writing style would make the poem extremely mar-ketable, she has not only *not* sold it but she told me she had not shared it with anyone outside of her family. Unlike almost all of the syllabic objects sold in the context of Cherokee tourism, and like the syllabary New Testament and hymnal, this graphic object was considered by its possessor to have real and powerful meaning.

An Intercultural Zone

In Cherokee tourism in the mid-1990s, semiotic potency, use-value, and exchange-value intersected in compelling ways. Syllabic objects were differentiated in terms of their semiotic use potential. The dis-tinction had to do with whether syllabic objects were considered to possess symbolic use-value, which, in the case of texts, meant that they were considered to have significant and specific meanings or perfor-mative powers. Those objects and texts in or on which the syllabary functioned as a true orthography were generally kept out of circulation as commodities, with the exception of language education materials. Other syllabic objects, in or on which the syllabary had been freed from specific semantic connections, were considered primarily to possess exchange-value as syllabary objects and were as free to enter the world of circulating commodities as any other objects. Those objects on which the syllabary was most mute and "useless" as *writing*—the mugs, key-chains, and so on—tended to be most useful as nontextual objects.

Syllabic writing has become increasingly visible in the Cherokee graphic landscape in the years since I did my fieldwork, during which time it has become more and more important to protect the community from the semiotic incursions associated with the new casino. Colorful syllabary signs appeared at the periphery of the Boundary in the past few years, attracting tourists and marking the enclosed space as a legitimate site for "cultural" tourism of a specifically Cherokee variety. Within the Boundary itself, the more bureaucratic syllabary signs continue the argument that this is an authentically Indian and Cherokee place, but they do more as well. These signs mark local spaces where most tourists may not even go, the infrastructural centers of the community. Should a tourist stumble upon these, they have the power to communicate that this community's cultural and linguistic legitimacy continues beyond the arena of tourism and into everyday life—that there is a living culture here, distinguishable from that of the mainstream United States. More important, they have the power to communicate this to members of the community itself.

In this intercultural zone that is Cherokee tourism, local boundaries and the community's identity and internal organization are all being negotiated. Access to various sources of linguistic (hence cultural) *value* is mediated by a variable assignment of *exchangeability*. Where the syllabary is most useful in the creation of meaningful texts (most symbolic in the Peircean sense), it is least exchangeable. However, other dimensions of the syllabary's semiotic usefulness, such as its iconic design potential, enhance exchange-value. The syllabary's role in tourism reinforces the linguistic and social world in which Cherokee language use and literacy are rare, valuable, and not necessarily suitable for widespread distribution.

There are also clear limits to the exchangeability of Cherokee culture considered more generally. Jokes about "five-dollar Indians" notwithstanding, the sale and purchase of Cherokee identity, cultural and legal, is perceived as a serious threat and no joking matter.[7]

Conclusion

Features of Eastern Cherokee Syllabic Literacy

It is clear that the Eastern Cherokee community of the mid-1990s treated the Cherokee syllabary in distinct ways in both thought and practice. Taken together, such treatment suggests the syllabary's great importance and culturally specific value to the local community, as well as a belief that its use should be limited to community members of the proper level of maturity who would use it for good purpose. Some of the patterns that emerged are listed below.

In a Nutshell: Treatment of the Syllabary

- In classrooms of all levels, and in the community at large, the syllabary was treated as a special and culturally specific writing system unlike other orthographies for writing English or Cherokee. The syllabary was also considered to have more inherent design potential than other writing systems, possibly due to both its perceived cultural iconicity and its perceived remoteness as a system for phonetic transcription.
- When it truly functioned in the most conventional sense as a writing system, that is, as a symbolic orthography, the syllabary was generally treated as a revelational medium. Whether the texts were Christian or medicinal, syllabary was seen uniquely as a point of access to truth and specialized knowledge in a way that other writing was not. This is part of what I sought to suggest in using the metaphor of the "code."

157

– The syllabary was not considered to be an arbitrary representation of sound but was seen as being uniquely connected to the Cherokee language. The potential transfer of this writing system to another language, for example, was not conceptually present in local language ideology.

– Some syllabary users saw the syllabary as a source of linguistic information about the Cherokee language, such as correct pronunciations.

– Some syllabary users saw the syllabary as being closely associated with "Western" dialect or biblical language.

While possession of syllabary-marked objects and a general familiarity with the syllabary were quite widespread, syllabary readers and writers made up a special subset of syllabary-using Cherokees. Some notable generalizations about syllabary users follow.

In a Nutshell: Syllabary Users

– Most Cherokees who knew the syllabary learned it as adults.

– Learning the syllabary was generally motivated either by a desire to preserve cultural heritage—to become a language teacher, for example—or in order to read the New Testament and hymnal in syllabary. A few Cherokees acknowledged that they were motivated to learn the syllabary out of a desire to read medicinal manuscripts.

– Many Cherokees who read the syllabary did not write, in the sense of producing new texts, in it. This trend probably reflects both the limited usefulness of writing Cherokee, given the small number of potential readers, and the association of handwritten Cherokee with medicine.

– Reading and writing syllabary had different connotations as practices, as did written and printed syllabary. Both the act of reading and printed syllabary were strongly associated with Christianity; the act of writing and handwritten syllabary were to some extent associated with medicine or "conjuring."

– Those Cherokees who did read syllabary usually were indexically marked as local cultural or religious experts. They were frequently Sunday school or Cherokee language teachers or producers of cultural material.

– Overall, the number of proficient syllabary readers remained fairly small. Literacy in the syllabary was treated as a specialization and also as an index of maturity.

Literacy: Practical Consciousness Made Tangible

One of the factors that makes Cherokee syllabic literacy unique, and indeed that makes each literacy unique, is its physical embodiment in specific, concrete spaces, objects, and human actions (see Fabian 1993). In our ethnographic accounts of specific literacies, it is important to account for the sensible experiences of users of writing systems—reading with eyes or fingers, hearing words read, tactile encounters with book covers and pages, training the hand to manipulate pen, chalk, or keyboard, and so on—and the tangible and circulable products of some literacy-related activities.

The presence of the syllabary in Eastern Cherokee life in the mid-1990s entailed a myriad of sensible experiences. Local potters used syllabary characters to mark clay pottery, even if they themselves did not read or write in the syllabary; these pots were then purchased and enjoyed for aesthetic as well as cultural reasons. Syllabary lettering and signs were used to assert the cultural legitimacy of social spaces in schools, at the annual Cherokee Fall Festival, and in the tourist-oriented downtown of Cherokee, North Carolina. The creative, physical act of singing a Cherokee hymn while holding a Cherokee hymnal (syllabary-only), whether or not one actually read the hymns, was an important practical (re)production of oneself as Cherokee and Christian. The material forms and corporeal experiences made locally meaningful through the syllabary's presence and use were diverse and numerous.

Cherokee writing is a mode of production of tangible cultural artifacts that effect meaning at all semiotic levels: symbolic, indexical, and iconic. But the relationship between the material dimensions of syllabary use and its iconic-indexical capacities is particularly important (cf. Urban 1996). Its visual qualities and impact, and its material contextual placement—these are the features of the syllabary that allow it to carry meaning beyond the conventional, symbolic level.

That is the "practical" side of "practical consciousness." On the "consciousness" side, it is clear that the practice of using a particular writing system within a given language community is affected by cultural beliefs and practices beyond the immediate contexts of writing and reading. In particular, users of the Cherokee syllabary (meaning those who had contact with the syllabary in any of its forms) treated various types of reading and writing (chiefly the reading and writing of printed versus handwritten syllabary but also of syllabic as opposed to alphabetic writing) as fundamentally different types of activities — so different, indeed, that they had the power to indexically characterize users as different types of readers and writers, from language and culture teachers to cultural experts, preachers, and medicine men. This typology reflects not only Cherokee beliefs about syllabic literacy but also some of the most important categories in the Cherokee social world.

Through the practices of writing, reading, and otherwise using a writing system and various texts, users revealed cultural assumptions not only concerning the relationships between written and spoken language and different categories of readers and writers but about the nature of knowledge. Various types of writing and reading indexed, and became metonymic substitutes for, various types of knowledge and information. Various kinds of users of written language also fell into different categories as people: what they knew, what they believed, various aspects of their perceived biological and cultural backgrounds, indeed part of who they were might be drawn by extension from the type of reader and writer they were. It is these *processes* of cultural identification and classification, perhaps more than the syllabary itself, that allow us to see a dynamic, living culture in action by studying syllabary usage.

Literacy as Communicative Practice

I have argued that the syllabary system, local ideologies of literacy, and patterns of syllabary use must all be studied to fully grasp what the Cherokee syllabary means in contemporary Eastern Cherokee life. It should be clear that local ideologies of literacy are not only supported and informed by patterned literacy practices. These ideologies in turn influence patterns of use and the way in which the writing system represents spoken language. For example, I noted in Chapter 4 that some medicine men, in the past, may have modified the system so as to narrow it as a system of transcription, drawing on a common belief that the system should encode accurately and completely and should possess the ability to obfuscate. Such modifications might be more widespread today if they did not conflict with another ideological belief concerning the syllabary—namely, that it is authoritatively codified in the New Testament, where no such modifications are made. In fact, as I discussed in Chapter 3, to write the syllabary idiosyncratically or with modification today would make one a target of suspicion.

Bible readers of various camps may also ultimately modify the way in which the syllabary is considered to represent spoken Cherokee. As I explained in Chapter 4, North Carolina Cherokees who encounter Western Cherokee phonemes in reading the Bible have three options when reading aloud. They may deliver the foreign pronunciation as is, in a kind of Bible-reading register; they may alter the pronunciation to make it phonemically Eastern; or they may substitute an entirely different lexical item. The second practice suggests that certain characters may be treated as though they represent one set of phonemes for Oklahoma speakers and a different set for North Carolina speakers. Were this practice to become widespread, it would alter the role of a subset of the syllabary's characters.

Taking a different route, some speakers have suggested the elimination of an entire set of syllabary characters (Figure 1, tenth row) that represent consonants not generally present in the dialect of North Carolina speakers—unless they are reading the Bible. Here again, were this to happen, a specific ideology of literacy asserting the belief that the syllabary should reflect an Eastern standard when used by Eastern speakers, and that characters unused in that standard should be eliminated, would be driving a fundamental change in the system itself.

Most dramatically, the emphasis placed on the correctness of syllabary ("spelling") pronunciations by some of those involved in language education and preservation may ultimately change not only the relationship between writing and language but even the spoken language itself, as books, rather than elderly speakers, come to serve as authoritative sources of information about the Cherokee language.

Structure at many levels—linguistic, cultural, social, and political—

emerges as the syllabary is used in diverse and complex ways. What allows corporeal practices like reading, writing, singing, wearing, possessing, and so on to re(produce) meaningful structural categories is belief, articulated or unarticulated. If the roles played by the syllabary in Cherokee education contribute to the division of the Cherokee community into a small group of mature specialists who know how to read and write syllabary and a large majority who do not, it is by way of linguistic ideologies about the syllabary's difficulty and unsuitability for most students, beliefs which are in turn supported by cultural presuppositions about the syllabary's status as a nonphonetic, culturally specific code.

The ideologies most relevant here are predominantly local ones. The picture I have painted of Cherokee literacy suggests the limited usefulness of an approach that would seek to read a larger, hegemonic ideological framework through the lens of literacy practices. In the case of Cherokee literacy in the syllabary, the potentially relevant "surrounding" ideologies are numerous, complex, and variable in origin. It would be wrong to argue that the syllabary was associated, even in its early years, with a monolithic and externally imposed ideology of progress and civilization.

In addition, the syllabary has always been one of a range of possible writing systems, not only for writing the Cherokee language but for writing in general as a Cherokee social practice. Thus it would be problematical to suggest that the ideologies associated with the *syllabary* and those associated with *literacy* in the Cherokee context are exactly the same. As we have seen, there is nothing so simple as a single Cherokee ideology of literacy, even as far as the syllabary is concerned. Handwriting, print, reading, copying, and other modes of interacting with the syllabary all have different implications.

The various ideologies of literacy that come into play in the context of syllabary usage are not only complex and multiple but intersect and overlap with ideologies of English-language literacy in interesting and significant ways. As I have pointed out, the Cherokee belief that easy phonetics constitute the most accessible and transparent Cherokee orthography rests on the culturally presupposed naturalness of English-language literacy. In addition, both the syllabary's perceived superiority as a design and its status as an index of Christian faith seem to rest to some extent on the contrast between the calligraphic style in which the syllabary is reproduced and the plainer style in which the similar capital roman letters are produced in writing English.

Locally articulated beliefs about the syllabary, such as the belief that the syllabary is a source of correct pronunciations yet at the same time flawed, or that it is closely linked to a Western dialect or to biblical language, would qualify as elements of language (or, more specifically, literacy) ideology. But note that these beliefs articulate with other, unstated cultural presuppositions. The syllabary's revelational character certainly supports its being intrinsically linked with biblical and other language, and its codelikeness helps us to understand why users value all the information it conveys, even extra vowels.

Language Use and Literacy as Icons of Community

The syllabary's role in Eastern Cherokee life certainly illustrates that language use and beliefs about language use may be mobilized in the definition or maintenance of a community, even when the majority of the community's members do not speak, read, or write the language. In the mid-1990s, beliefs and practices related to syllabary usage contributed to the vision and enactment of particular models of community.

Reading and writing skills were distributed among a limited number of specialists positioned throughout the community in key social roles. As I indicated, this positioning points to the existence of a different order of community than a superficial glance at Eastern Cherokee geopolitics and bureaucracy would suggest. Although the near total circulation and consumption of the Eastern Band's English-language newspaper might suggest an Andersonian (1984) homogeneity to the community, the distribution of syllabary paints a different picture, one in which differentiation based on age, cultural expertise, and religious experience figures large, and in which the most important unit may be one's own church or Cherokee subcommunity. The community's English-language literacy suggests, or serves as a metaphor for, a different model of community than does the distribution of Cherokee language literacy.

The distribution of various types of syllabary-marked signs and commodities marks out realms of variable semiotic accessibility on the reservation. Where the syllabary was most visible it was least functional as a symbolic orthography. This system protected the most semantically charged uses of the syllabary and, generally speaking, kept it out of the realm of commodification. Individuals, such as the school children who teased me in the community's public library, also used the syllabary to mark off boundaries and to index their in-group status.

The configuration of another notion of community, composed of speakers and nonspeakers alike, grew around a set of beliefs about a particular Cherokee dialect. The perceived existence of this Eastern standard, the *kituhwa* dialect, suggested a cultural hierarchy among Eastern speakers and also a parity between East and West.

The community's boundaries were in part negotiated via the intercultural zone of tourism. But the tourist scene in Cherokee was also the site where many tensions *internal* to Cherokee cultural self-representation were worked out. How to represent the syllabary—as a feature of civilization, Indianness, or both, and whether to naturalize or pan-Indianize Cherokee culture to make it more appealing to tourists or as a logical complement to the national park—these were all questions being worked out within and by this community itself. We know this because these issues of self-representation extended beyond the context of tourism into other areas of Cherokee life, such as language education and cultural preservation. Of course, tourists did supply the demand for the pan-Indian and for images of the natural. And they were partners with the local community in the process of cultural commodification. But I have stressed the meanings and limits of commodification from the Cherokee side to emphasize the point that the Eastern Cherokees are *not* culturally impoverished victims of tourism. In the course of the sensible experiences of daily life, this community is outlined, given shape, and its locally significant categories are reproduced by its members, even while it appears that the community is accommodating itself to the dominant society, and even while it is subject to intense contact with and scrutiny by outsiders.

Signs of the Times

The Cherokee syllabary is still very much in use—in Cherokee language education, in churches, in Cherokee newspapers and other publications, as a symbol of national pride, and in a variety of less formal ways—but the patterns of usage, associated ideologies, and even the ways in which the syllabary represents speech have not remained static since the nineteenth century. Nor have they remained the same since the research that informs this book was carried out. I have sought here to document the vitality and flux of this system in use at a particular moment in history.

Studying beliefs about reading and writing and the embodiment of those beliefs through the practical activities we call literacy provides a window into a given community's wider beliefs about language, knowledge, communication, and representation and its own articulation with the dominant society and its media. The Cherokees' extremely rich history of literacy provides a special opportunity in this regard, but all of us whose semiotic worlds include "talking leaves"[1] participate every day in a similarly complex process of self-representation, self-transformation, and negotiation of individual and shared identities and boundaries.

Notes

Introduction

1. For detailed discussion of the Peircean semiotic categories of symbol, index, and icon and illustrations of their use, see Duranti 1997, Hanks 2000, Hartshorne and Weiss 1931, Mannheim 2000, Mertz and Parmentier 1985, Parmentier 1987, and Silverstein 1976.

2. For discussions of U.S. standard language ideology and the subordination of nonstandard dialects and languages and the people who speak them, see Silverstein 1995 and Lippi-Green 1997.

3. There are many excellent sources on Cherokee history for readers wishing to learn more than is presented in this very brief summary. For example, see Anderson 1991; Finger 1984, 1991; Hill 1997; McLoughlin 1986; Mooney 1982; and Perdue 1979, 1998.

4. For varied and interesting perspectives on the Eastern Band in recent years, see Finger 1991, French and Hornbuckle 1981, Hill 1997, Hipps 1994, Lefler 1996, and Neely 1991. Of these, Neely's is the only general ethnographic treatment, but it focuses on one of the reservation's subcommunities rather than on the Eastern Band as a whole.

Chapter One

1. Even the syllabary's "vowel" characters (the first line of the chart in Figure 1) may be analyzed as glottal stop + vowel; hence they, too, represent consonant-vowel combinations.

As there are numerous good sources on the syllabary's history (e.g., Foreman 1938; Foster 1885, 1899; Kilpatrick 1965; McLoughlin 1986; and Perdue 1994), what follows will be a brief summary.

2. In a phonetic system, characters represent distinguishable sounds (e.g., consonants or vowels). In a logographic system, characters represent words.

In an ideographic system, characters represent ideas. Finally, in a pictographic system, pictures (more or less abstracted) convey meaning. The suggestion that Sequoyah's earliest invention was a nonphonetic system makes possible a linkage between Sequoyan writing and Indian "picture writing" or other presumed systems of pan-Indian written communication. Traveller Bird (1971) may be drawing on this potential linkage in his assertions that the syllabary predates Sequoyah and that it was used for intertribal communication. Evidence of this linkage can be seen in contemporary usage as well, for example in T-shirt and postcard designs that combine syllabic writing with pictographic design. As I argue in later chapters, these types of combinations help lend the syllabary its codelike quality.

3. For example, in a 1967 protest against a tourist attraction called "Cherokee Village," Cherokees in Tahlequah, Oklahoma, picketed the facility's grand opening holding signs lettered in Cherokee (Five County Cherokee Organization 1968). Since the intended audience consisted largely of non-Cherokee-speaking local bureaucrats and their invited guests, the signs were not intended only to be communicative in the straightforward sense, but were also symbolic representations of Cherokee achievements and pride, alienation from the local white administrators, and cultural distance created through illegibility.

4. Butrick, a missionary to the Cherokees, collected extensive cultural information, some of which is contained in his *Antiquities of the Cherokee Indians* (1884). Boudinot was a Cherokee who received a formal education at the Indian school at Cornwall, Connecticut, became editor of the *Cherokee Phoenix* in 1828, and was assassinated in 1839 in retaliation for signing the Treaty of New Echota, which authorized the Cherokee removal to the West.

5. There are dissenting voices. Traveller Bird (1971) asserts that the syllabary, a long-standing tool of Indian warrior-scribes, predated Sequoyah by hundreds of years. *Both* this story and the story of the miraculous invention require a leap of faith.

6. Payne was a poet who collected extensive historical and cultural data on the Cherokees, much of which, still unpublished, is in the Newberry Library in Chicago. Payne was arrested by the Georgia guard in 1835 while in the company of the Cherokee leader John Ross, an opponent of removal (Mooney 1982: 122).

7. The relationship between the syllabary and Cherokee medicine or conjuring was later to become important. Once it became the accepted norm to write medicinal or conjuring texts in the syllabary, learning to read and write syllabary became a requirement for becoming an "Indian doctor" (Gulick 1960: 97).

8. Most anthropologists today prefer the word "consultant" over the older

term "informant" for at least two reasons. The new term better reflects the advisory or teaching role played by those we work with in the field, and it does not carry the potentially negative connotations (e.g., from law enforcement) of "informant."

9. John Ross, leader of the unsuccessful opposition to removal, served as principal chief of the Cherokee Nation in the East from 1828 until the removal and in the West from 1839 until his death in 1866.

10. Pickering's orthography and his analysis of Cherokee phonology may be found in Krueger 1963: 30–33. For the missionary Samuel A. Worcester's take on the similarities and differences between Sequoyah's syllabary and Pickering's orthography, see Kilpatrick and Kilpatrick 1968: 5–9.

11. Worcester acted as missionary to the Cherokees beginning in 1825. He worked to establish the syllabary type and printing press to be used in the production of the *Cherokee Phoenix* and was responsible for the translation into Cherokee and publication of numerous texts. Worcester was responsible for the presentation of the syllabary in the now ubiquitous chart that first appeared in the *Phoenix* (Figure 1). Worcester's commitment to the Cherokees was unflagging. He was imprisoned twice in the course of the Eastern Cherokee Nation's struggle with the state of Georgia (Mooney 1982: 217–18).

12. Foreman's books formed an important component of the University of Oklahoma Press series "The Civilization of the American Indian."

13. Fogelson (1974: 108) has pointed out the "implicit racist assumption" of this assertion.

14. Although the reservees were supposed to meet basic standards entitling them to citizenship, such as literacy and reliance on agriculture, these traits characterized the reservees to varying degrees, with those in the Middle (mountain) town areas being seen as little more "civilized" than their ancestors (Riggs 1988). In fact, few of these reservees actually received the promised land, and none received citizenship during the nineteenth century.

Chapter Two

1. One informal local survey suggested that as few as 7 percent of resident enrollees may speak Cherokee, but this may reflect the specificity of the surveyed sample because the survey was distributed only to tribal school employees.

2. Research suggests that early childhood bilingualism actually enhances language and other academic skills (see, e.g., McCarty and Watahomigie 1999 and Smith and Arnot-Hopffer 1998).

3. I refer to this and two other local systems for writing Cherokee as "pho-

netics" because that is how they are locally described. In that the syllabary represents the sounds of speech, rather than whole words or concepts, the syllabary could also be described as "phonetic," but that is not how it is characterized locally.

4. See Figure 1.

5. There is a phonemic difference based on aspiration between [tsa] or [tʃa] on the one hand and [tsha] or [tʃha] on the other, whereas the difference in point of articulation in each case is generally considered a dialectal matter. In other words, [tsa] and [tʃa] (both unaspirated affricates, the first alveolar and the second postalveolar) are considered to be two dialectal variants of the same phoneme. The [s] or [ʃ] may also be voiced in some contexts.

6. I was surprised to see this spelling of this word. The substitution of the "tla" for ⟨hla⟩ suggests a pronunciation probably more common in Oklahoma than in North Carolina. Some North Carolina speakers have even suggested that the syllabary row containing ⟨Ɫ⟩, ⟨tla⟩ be eliminated in the North Carolina context.

7. The colors being written are *atse:ʔi*, 'green'; *une:ka*, 'white'; *kikake*, 'red'; *sakho:nike*, 'blue'; *uwo:tike*, 'brown'; and *talo:nike*, 'yellow.'

8. In the classroom, I never heard the learning or preservation of traditional medical or magical knowledge, particularly that found in *itikewesti* manuscripts, mentioned as a motivation for learning the syllabary. In this context, at least, the reading of formulas was not overtly recognized as a potential application of syllabary literacy. This picture differs somewhat from that encountered by Raymond D. Fogelson in the late 1950s, when, he reports, "a few conservatives were motivated to learn syllabary to become medicine men or to be able to use inherited manuscripts" (Fogelson, pers. com., May 1995). Although the link between the syllabary and local plants remained salient, as illustrated by the semantic emphases of syllabary educational materials, the medicinal and magical uses of those plants were excluded from classroom discourse.

9. The lexical associations of the syllabary in these contexts also suggests a presupposition of "naturalness." Culturally valued plants and animals, a significant part of the Cherokee cultural landscape, were also considered to be "natural." See later discussion on the presupposed naturalness of the syllabary as a writing system.

Chapter Three

1. More recently, I have seen another easy phonetic spelling in a public sign. The sign for a hotel in downtown Cherokee welcomed visitors for a time with the greeting "si-yough" (*siyo;* 'hello').

2. According to most fluent North Carolina Cherokee speakers, *tsalaki* is not a place name but refers only to the Cherokee people or language. Downtown "Cherokee," the business and tourism center of the reservation, is the community of *e:lawo:ti* or Yellowhill. Possible explanations for the presence of the word *tsalaki* include the influence of Oklahoma speakers, who sometimes refer to the North Carolina reservation as *tsalaki u:we:thi,* 'Old Cherokee,' and the much greater familiarity of the word *tsalaki,* as opposed to *e:lawo:ti,* to students and readers.

The quoted text translates as 'One day the bear was walking and he saw a mouse. The mouse said hello, I live in Cherokee, do you?'

3. See Walker and Sarbaugh (1993) for an illustration of Sequoyah's original orthography and order of presentation. Local attitudes toward this order, as compared with the order in Worcester's chart, will be discussed in the next chapter.

4. While approximately half of the characters as printed (or more, depending on how rigid one's criteria are) seem to resemble roman letters or arabic numerals, this was probably less true in Sequoyah's original, handwritten versions (Walker and Sarbaugh 1993). Other of the printed characters may seem to resemble Greek or other alphabetic characters, but the same caution applies. Some of the characters are difficult for those literate in English to distinguish because they are variants (upside down, backward, modified by the addition of a line or slash) on what appears to be a single roman character.

5. Again, see Walker and Sarbaugh (1993) for Sequoyah's original orthography.

6. Many readers are probably familiar with the famous Navajo code-talkers, but they may not be aware that other Native Americans played this role during World War II as well. At the Comanche Tribal Complex in Lawton, Oklahoma, for example, a photograph of Comanche code-talkers is on display and information about their service is available on the Comanche Nation's web page. See ⟨http://members.tripod.com/~Quohadi/code.html⟩.

Chapter Four

1. In hymn singing, however, such pronunciations are routine. This is not unlike singers of hymns in English delivering spelling pronunciations for words such as "look-ed" that would rarely be heard even in the most careful English speech.

2. How spelling conventions are established in Cherokee is a matter that deserves some attention. If speakers are aware that a particular word occurs in the Bible, that would certainly be considered the source of the conventional, and standard, spelling, unless the spelling was dialect-specific, in which case

the matter would become somewhat more complicated. Commonly spelled words have conventional spellings that have probably been regularized by the small pool of language teachers, many of whom were trained in the syllabary at the same time. If the word cannot be found in the Bible, one consultant told me, "it's part of your own discretion, as to how you've heard it, as to what syllable you're gonna use."

3. The Overhill dialect is referred to by a number of Eastern Cherokees, straight-facedly, as the "Over-the-Hill" dialect.

4. Raymond Fogelson (pers. com., May 1995) notes that this is similar to the way traditional formulas are treated. A precise and unerring delivery is necessary to ensure efficacy. It has also been suggested that the immutability attributed to the Cherokee New Testament parallels the immutability commonly attributed to the King James Bible by users of that text.

5. *Kituhwa*, known as a Cherokee mother town, was located near present-day Bryson City, North Carolina. The Eastern Band recently purchased the private land on which lies the central mound structure of *Kituhwa*. Although the land has been plowed over for generations, a slight rise at the mound site is still visible. A brief excavation recently conducted by the Eastern Band revealed one of the most artifact-rich sites in all of preremoval Cherokee country (Lisa J. Lefler, pers. com., 1998). *Kituhwa* is also the name of the religious stomp dance society in Oklahoma and in North Carolina. In that context, it is usually spelled ⟨Keetoowah⟩. In addition, there is a political entity, the United Keetoowah Band, which has federal recognition as a Cherokee tribe in Oklahoma separate from the Cherokee Nation.

6. This word was rewritten to reflect a phonemic difference between most Oklahoma and most North Carolina speakers. However, the word, not commonly spoken in North Carolina at all, remains. In ordinary North Carolina Cherokee speech, 'not' is *ke* or *kehsti*.

7. The titles of hymns are in English, in the hymnal itself, even though the songs are only in syllabary. The title frequently assists the singers in locating the corresponding tune, such as "Amazing Grace," and does not always pertain to the meaning of the song in Cherokee.

8. It is possible that a different picture would emerge in Oklahoma. The two Oklahoma speakers who were Cherokee language teachers during my field study did not use the syllabary, while many local language teachers did. It may be that because the speaking population is so much smaller in Cherokee, there is much more importance placed on using the syllabary as a marker of proficiency.

9. As an example, see the comments of elementary school Teacher 3 in Chapter 3.

10. This local treatment of the syllables as morphemes was pointed out to me by Michael Silverstein (pers. com., 12 May 1995).

11. See Walker and Sarbaugh (1993). Although the authors argue that Sequoyah continued to be responsible for the *shape* of the characters, even after Worcester became involved with the syllabary, there is no suggestion that Sequoyah himself ever took to using Worcester's phonetic chart.

12. See Long's chart, reproduced in the back of Chiltoskey (1972). Reading each column top to bottom, and then moving left to right, it reproduces the original Sequoyan order.

13. The belief in this (unknown) pattern is shared by Raymond D. Fogelson (pers. com., 1994).

Chapter Five

1. Although I did not observe this myself, I have been told that women sometimes also work in the same capacity as Cherokee "princesses" (Lisa J. Lefler, pers. com., September 1999). These "princesses" posing for tourists are not to be confused with those individuals holding the respected local titles of "Miss Cherokee" and "Little Miss Cherokee," who are tribal dignitaries and cultural ambassadors.

2. Tourists sometimes become irritated when what they take to be traditionally "Indian" either is not available or turns out not to be locally made. In a local restaurant, I once overheard tourists complaining that what had been described to them as a typical Indian meal did not include frybread. What they were actually eating was bean bread, a boiled dumpling-like bread made of cornmeal and pinto beans. Bean bread is about as "authentically" Cherokee a food as there is, in the spectrum of currently available foods, and it is often eaten at predominantly Cherokee gatherings like church singings and local fund-raisers. Frybread is a much more widely known, pan-Indian staple available at powwows across the country, especially in the Midwest.

I heard about another tourist who told her son she would not buy the plastic tomahawk he wanted from a gift shop because it was just "cheap junk." It wasn't even local, she pointed out, reading the label—it was "Made in Taiwan." Exasperated with this customer (who evidently felt that mass-produced plastic replicas of weapons not even indigenous to the area *should* be locally made), the Cherokee salesperson told her she was mistaken. Certainly the tomahawk was locally made; it was from Taiwan Creek, just up the mountain. In her desperation for local authenticity, the tourist bought it (Lisa J. Lefler, pers. com., September 1999).

3. The word "naturalization" has many meanings as used in scholarly writ-

ing about culture and language. What I mean here by saying that the syllabary is naturalized is that it is made to seem a part of nature or emergent from the natural environment.

4. The reader will recognize *kituhwa* as the name of the Cherokee dialect spoken by most North Carolina Cherokees and as the name for a traditional Cherokee religious community. The planners of this pan-Indian event clearly sought to highlight the proximity and participation of the Eastern Band in choosing this name.

5. Whether or not this is true could be confirmed to a certain extent by comparing the numbers of enrollment applications received by various tribes, but this method would not capture the number of people who assert a Cherokee identity without even attempting to enroll.

6. Though it is nearly impossible to imagine the plan working as described, this event and the way the story is told show how important protection of the Cherokees' rich linguistic heritage is taken to be and how immediate the perceived threats against it.

7. "Five-dollar Indians" are non-Indians who, at the time of tribal enrollment, reportedly paid a small sum to be admitted to the tribal rolls.

Conclusion

1. Sequoyah is believed to have called written pages "talking leaves."

References

Adams, Kathleen M. 1995. "Making-Up the Toraja? The Appropriation of Tourism, Anthropology, and Museums for Politics in Upland Sulawesi, Indonesia." *Ethnology* 34:143–53.

Anderson, Benedict. 1983. *Imagined Communities.* London: Verso.

Anderson, William L., ed. 1991. *Cherokee Removal: Before and After.* Athens: University of Georgia Press.

Bauman, Richard. 1991. Remarks Delivered as Discussant at the 90th Annual Meeting of the American Anthropological Association, 20–24 November, Chicago.

Besnier, Niko. 1991. "Literacy and the Notion of Person on Nukulaelae Atoll." *American Anthropologist* 93:570–87.

Bloomfield, Leonard. 1964. "Literate and Illiterate Speech." In *Language in Culture and Society,* edited by Dell Hymes, 391–96. New York: Harper & Row.

Boyarin, Jonathan, ed. 1993. *The Ethnography of Reading.* Berkeley: University of California Press.

Brody, Jill. 1996. "The New Literacy." *Journal of Linguistic Anthropology* 6:96–104.

Brown, John P. 1938. *Old Frontiers: The Story of the Cherokee Indians from Earliest Times to the Date of Their Removal.* Kingsport, Tenn.: Southern Publishers.

Butrick, Daniel S. 1884. *Antiquities of the Cherokee Indians.* Vinita, Indian Territory: Indian Chieftan.

Castañeda, Uetzil E. 1996. *In the Museum of Maya Culture: Touring Chichén Itzá.* Minneapolis: University of Minnesota Press.

Chafe, Wallace L., and Jack Frederick Kilpatrick. 1963. "Inconsistencies in Cherokee Spelling." In *Symposium on Language and Culture: Proceedings of the 1962 Annual Spring Meeting of the American Ethnological Society,* edited by Viola E. Garfield, 60–63. Seattle: American Ethnological Society.

Chiltoskey, Mary Ulmer. 1972. *Cherokee Words with Pictures*. Asheville, N.C.: Gilbert Printing Company.

Comaroff, Jean, and John L. Comaroff. 1991. *Of Revelation and Revolution: Christianity, Colonialism, and Consciousness in South Africa*. Chicago: University of Chicago Press.

Cook, William Hinton. 1979. "A Grammar of North Carolina Cherokee." Ph.D. diss., Yale University.

Davis, Elizabeth E. 1999. "Metamorphosis in the Culture Market of Niger." *American Anthropologist* 101:485–501.

Desjarlais, Robert. 1996. "The Office of Reason: On the Politics of Language and Agency in a Shelter for 'the Homeless Mentally Ill.' " *American Ethnologist* 23:880–900.

Duranti, Alessandro. 1997. "Indexical Speech across Samoan Communities." *American Anthropologist* 99(2):342–54.

Eckert, Penelope, and Sally McConnell-Ginet. 1992. "Think Practically and Look Locally: Language and Gender as Community-Based Practice." *Annual Review of Anthropology* 21:461–90.

Eisenstein, Elizabeth. 1979. *The Printing Press as an Agent of Change*. Cambridge: Cambridge University Press.

Errington, Frederick, and Deborah Gewertz. 1989. "Tourism and Anthropology in a Post-Modern World." *Oceania* 60:37–54.

Fabian, Johannes. 1993. "Keep Listening: Ethnography and Reading." In *The Ethnography of Reading*, edited by Jonathan Boyarin, 80–97. Berkeley: University of California Press.

Febvre, Lucien, and Henri-Jean Martin. 1958. *The Coming of the Book: The Impact of Printing, 1450–1800*. London: NLB.

Feeling, Durbin, and William Pulte. 1975. *Cherokee-English Dictionary*. Tahlequah: Cherokee Nation of Oklahoma.

Finger, John R. 1984. *The Eastern Band of Cherokees, 1819–1900*. Knoxville: University of Tennessee Press.

———. 1991. *Cherokee Americans: The Eastern Band of Cherokees in the Twentieth Century*. Lincoln: University of Nebraska Press.

Five County Cherokee Organization. 1968. "First Cherokee Picket Line Surprises Village Guests." *Indian Voices:*13–15.

Fogelson, Raymond D. 1974. "On the Varieties of Indian History: Sequoyah and Traveller Bird." *Journal of Ethnic Studies* 2:105–12.

———. 1980. "The Conjuror in Eastern Society." *Journal of Cherokee Studies* 5: 60–87.

Fogelson, Raymond D., and Paul Kutsche. 1961. "Cherokee Economic Cooperatives: The Gadugi." In *Symposium on Cherokee and Iroquois Culture*, edited by

William N. Fenton and John Gulick, 88–98. Bureau of American Ethnology, Bulletin 180. Washington, D.C.: Smithsonian Institution.

Foreman, Grant. 1934. *The Five Civilized Tribes*. Norman: University of Oklahoma Press.

———. 1938. *Sequoyah*. Norman: University of Oklahoma Press.

Foster, George E. 1885. *Se-Quo-Yah, the American Cadmus and Modern Moses*. Philadelphia: Office of the Indian Rights Association.

———. 1899. *Story of the Cherokee Bible*. Ithaca, N.Y.: Democrat Press.

French, Laurence, and Jim Hornbuckle, eds. 1981. *The Cherokee Perspective*. Boone, N.C.: Appalachian Consortium Press.

Friday, Sarah. 1998. "Saving Grace." *Southern Living* (March): 14CL–17CL.

Gaillard, Frye, and Carolyn DeMeritt. 1998. *As Long as the Waters Flow: Native Americans in the South and the East*. Winston-Salem, N.C.: John F. Blair.

Gilbert, William Harlan. 1978. *The Eastern Cherokees*. Bureau of American Ethnology Bulletin 133, Anthropological Papers 23. 1943. Reprint, New York: AMS Press.

Goody, Jack, ed. 1968. "Introduction." In *Literacy in Traditional Societies*, edited by Jack Goody, 1–26. Cambridge: Cambridge University Press.

———. 1977. *The Domestication of the Savage Mind*. Cambridge: Cambridge University Press.

Goody, Jack, and Ian Watt. 1972. "The Consequences of Literacy." In *Language and Social Context*, edited by Pier P. Giglioli, 311–57. 1963. Reprint, New York: Penguin Books.

Grooms, Don, and John Oocumma. 1989. *How to Talk Trash in Cherokee*. Gainesville, Fla.: Downhome.

Gulick, John. 1973. *Cherokees at the Crossroads*. Chapel Hill: University of North Carolina Press.

Halverson, John. 1992. "Goody and the Implosion of the Literacy Thesis." *Man* 27(2):301–17.

Hanks, William F. 1996. *Language and Communicative Practices*. Boulder: Westview Press.

———. 2000. "Indexicality." *Journal of Linguistic Anthropology* 9(1–2):124–26.

Harbsmeier, Michael. 1989. "Writing and the Other: Travellers' Literacy, or Towards an Archaeology of Orality." In *Literacy and Society*, edited by Karen Schousboe and Mogens Trolle Larsen, 197–228. Copenhagen: Akademisk Forlag.

Harkin, Michael, and Sergei Kan. 1996. "Special Issue: Native American Women's Responses to Christianity." *Ethnohistory* 43.

Hartshorne, Charles, and Paul Weiss, eds. 1931. *The Collected Papers of Charles Sanders Peirce*. Cambridge, Mass.: Belknap Press.

Havelock, Eric A. 1976. *Origins of Western Literacy.* Toronto: Ontario Institute of Education.

Heath, Shirley Brice. 1983. *Ways with Words: Language, Life, and Work in Communities and Classrooms.* Cambridge: Cambridge University Press.

Hill, Sarah H. 1997. *Weaving New Worlds: Southeastern Cherokee Women and Their Basketry.* Chapel Hill: University of North Carolina Press.

Hipps, Doris Bradley. 1994. "The Eastern Band of Cherokees: A Study of Their Perceptions of Education and Dropping Out of School." Ed.D. thesis, University of South Carolina.

Holmes, Ruth Bradley, and Betty Sharp Smith. 1977. *Beginning Cherokee.* 1976. Reprint, Norman: University of Oklahoma Press.

Kaestle, Carl F. 1985. "The History of Literacy and the History of Readers." *Review of Research in Education* 12:1–53.

Kahn, Miriam. 2000. "Tahiti Intertwined: Ancestral Land, Tourist Postcard, and Nuclear Test Site." *American Anthropologist* 102:7–26.

Kilpatrick, Jack Frederick. 1965. *Sequoyah of Earth and Intellect.* Austin: Encino Press.

Kilpatrick, Jack Frederick, and Anna Gritts Kilpatrick. 1965. *The Shadow of Sequoyah: Social Documents of the Cherokees, 1862–1964.* Norman: University of Oklahoma Press.

————. 1970. *Notebook of a Cherokee Shaman.* Washington, D.C.: Smithsonian Institution Press.

————, eds. 1968. *New Echota Letters: Contributions of Samuel A. Worcester to the Cherokee Phoenix.* Dallas: Southern Methodist University Press.

King, Duane. 1975. "A Grammar and Dictionary of the Cherokee Language." Ph.D. diss., University of Georgia.

Krueger, John R. 1963. "Two Early Grammars of Cherokee." *Anthropological Linguistics* 5:1–57.

Leap, William L. 1991. "Pathways and Barriers to Indian Language Literacy-Building on the Northern Ute Reservation." *Anthropology and Education Quarterly* 22:21–41.

Lefler, Lisa J. 1996. "Mentorship as an Intervention Strategy in Relapse Reduction among Native American Youth." Ph.D. diss., University of Tennessee.

Lippi-Green, Rosina. 1997. *English with an Accent: Language, Ideology and Discrimination in the United States.* London: Routledge.

Mannheim, Bruce. 2000. "Iconicity." *Journal of Linguistic Anthropology* 9(1–2): 107–10.

Marx, Karl. 1977. *Capital.* Vol. 1. New York: Vintage Books.

Marx, Karl, and Friedrich Engels. 1970. *The German Ideology: Part One.* New York: International Publishers.

McCarty, Teresa L., and Lucille J. Watahomigie. 1999. "Reclaiming Indigenous Languages." *Common Ground: Archeology and Ethnography in the Public Interest* (Fall):32–43.

McLoughlin, William G. 1986. *Cherokee Renascence in the New Republic.* Princeton: Princeton University Press.

Mertz, Elizabeth, and Richard J. Parmentier, eds. 1985. *Semiotic Mediation: Sociocultural and Psychological Perspectives.* Orlando: Academic Press.

Mooney, James. 1892. "Improved Cherokee Alphabets." *American Anthropologist* 5:63–64.

———. 1982. *Myths of the Cherokee and Sacred Formulas of the Cherokees.* U.S. Bureau of American Ethnology Bulletins 7 and 19. 1891, 1900. Reprint, Cherokee, N.C.: Cherokee Heritage Books.

Mooney, James, and Frans M. Olbrechts, eds. 1932. *The Swimmer Manuscript: Cherokee Sacred Formulas and Medicinal Prescriptions.* Washington, D.C.: Smithsonian Institution.

Nash, Dennison. 1989. "Tourism as a Form of Imperialism." In *Hosts and Guests: The Anthropology of Tourism,* edited by Valene L. Smith, 37–52. 1977. Reprint, Philadelphia: University of Pennsylvania Press.

Neely, Sharlotte. 1991. *Snowbird Cherokees: People of Persistence.* Athens: University of Georgia Press.

Newman, Aryeh. 1996. "The Oral and Written Interface: Some Talmudic Evidence." *Language and Communication* 16:153–64.

Ochs, Elinor, and Alessandro Duranti. 1986. "Literacy Instruction in a Samoan Village." In *The Acquisition of Literacy: Ethnographic Perspectives,* edited by Bambi Schieffelin and Perry Gilmore, 213–32. Norwood, N.J.: Ablex.

Ong, Walter. 1982. *Orality and Literacy: The Technologizing of the Word.* London: Methuen.

Parmentier, Richard J. 1987. "Peirce Divested for Non-Intimates." *RSSI* 7:19–37.

Pennington, Daniel, and Robert Bushyhead. 1994. *Cherokee A-B-C Coloring Book with Words in English and Cherokee.* Cherokee, N.C.: Cherokee Publications.

Perdue, Theda. 1977. "Rising from the Ashes: The *Cherokee Phoenix* as an Ethnohistorical Source." *Ethnohistory* 24:207–18.

———. 1979. *Slavery and the Evolution of Cherokee Society, 1540–1866.* Knoxville: University of Tennessee Press.

———. 1983. *Cherokee Editor: The Writings of Elias Boudinot.* Knoxville: University of Tennessee Press.

———. 1994. "The Sequoyah Syllabary and Cultural Revitalization." In *Perspectives on the Southeast: Linguistics, Archaeology, and Ethnohistory,* edited by Patricia B. Kwachka, 116–25. Athens: University of Georgia Press.

————. 1998. *Cherokee Women: Gender and Culture Change, 1700-1835.* Lincoln: University of Nebraska Press.

Philips, Susan U. 1998. "Language Ideologies in Institutions of Power: A Commentary." In *Language Ideologies: Practice and Theory,* edited by K. A. Woolard, B. B. Schieffelin, and P. V. Kroskrity, 211-25. New York: Oxford University Press.

Reddy, Marlita A., ed. 1993. *Statistical Record of Native North Americans.* Detroit: Gale.

Riggs, Brett H. 1988. "An Historical and Archaeological Reconnaissance of Citizen Cherokee Reservations in Macon, Swain, and Jackson Counties, North Carolina." Raleigh: North Carolina Division of Archives and History.

Sahlins, Marshall. 1993. "Goodbye to *Tristes Tropes:* Ethnography in the Context of Modern World History." *Journal of Modern History* 65:1-25.

Saussure, Ferdinand de. 1966. *Course in General Linguistics.* 1959. Reprint, New York: McGraw Hill.

Scancarelli, Janine. 1992. "Aspiration and Cherokee Orthographies." In *The Linguistics of Literacy,* edited by Pamela Downing, Susan D. Lima, and Michael Noonan, 135-52. Amsterdam: John Benjamins.

————. 1996a. "Cherokee Writing." In *The World's Writing Systems,* edited by P. T. Daniels and W. Bright Daniels, 587-602. New York: Oxford University Press.

————. 1996b. "Learning to Write in the Cherokee Syllabary." In *1994 Mid-America Linguistics Conference Papers.* Lawrence: Department of Linguistics, University of Kansas.

Scribner, Sylvia, and Michael Cole. 1981. *The Psychology of Literacy.* Cambridge, Mass.: Harvard University Press.

Sears, James, and Doris B. Hipps. N.d. "Clinics but No Curriculum: The Case of the Booger Dance and the Keetoowah Curriculum." Unpublished ms.

Silverstein, Michael. 1976. "Shifters, Linguistic Categories and Cultural Description." In *Meaning in Anthropology,* edited by Keith H. Basso and Henry A. Selby, 11-55. Santa Fe: School of American Research.

————. 1979. "Language Structure and Linguistic Ideology." In *The Elements: A Parasession on Linguistic Units and Levels,* edited by Paul R. Clyne et al., 193-247. Chicago: Chicago Linguistic Society.

————. 1994. "Whorfianism and the Linguistic Imagination of Nationality." Paper Presented at the Advanced Seminar on "Language Ideologies" at the School of American Research, 24 April, Santa Fe, N.M.

————. 1995. "Language and the Culture of Gender: At the Intersection of Structure, Usage and Ideology." In *Language, Culture and Society,* edited by Ben G. Blount, 513-50. 1985. Reprint, Prospect Heights, Ill.: Waveland Press.

————. 1996. "Monoglot 'Standard' in America: Standardization and Meta-phors of Linguistic Hegemony." In *The Matrix of Language: Contemporary Linguistic Anthropology*, edited by D. Brenneis and R. H. S. Macaulay Bren-neis, 284–306. Boulder: Westview Press.

Smith, Patrick H., and Elizabeth Arnot-Hopffer. 1998. "Exito Bilingüe: Pro-moting Spanish Literacy in a Dual Language Immersion Program." *Bilingual Research Journal* 22:261–77.

Smith, Valene L., ed. 1989. *Hosts and Guests: The Anthropology of Tourism*. Phila-delphia: University of Pennsylvania Press.

Soltow, Lee, and Edward Stevens. 1981. *The Rise of Literacy and the Common School in the United States: A Socioeconomic Analysis to 1870*. Chicago: Univer-sity of Chicago Press.

Starkey, Marion L. 1946. *The Cherokee Nation*. New York: Knopf.

Street, Brian V. 1984. *Literacy in Theory and Practice*. Cambridge: Cambridge University Press.

————, ed. 1993. *Cross-Cultural Approaches to Literacy*. Cambridge: Cambridge University Press.

Tax, Sol, and Robert K. Thomas. 1968. "An Experiment in Cross-Cultural Edu-cation, 1962–67, Report of the University of Chicago." In *Hearings before a Special Subcommittee on Indian Education of the Senate Committee on Labor and Public Welfare, on the Study of the Education of Indian Children*, 940–58. Washington, D.C.: U.S. Government Printing Office.

Traveller Bird. 1971. *Tell Them They Lie: The Sequoyah Myth*. Los Angeles: West-ernlore.

Turner, Terence. 1984. "Value, Production, and Exploitation in Non-Capitalist Societies." Paper Presented at the Symposium "Culture and Historical Ma-terialism" at the 83rd Annual Meeting of the American Anthropological Association, Denver.

Urban, Greg. 1996. *Metaphysical Community: The Interplay of the Senses and the Intellect*. Austin: University of Texas Press.

U.S. Bureau of the Census. 1990a. *Census of Population (1990). General Population Characteristics. North Carolina*. Washington, D.C.: U.S. Government Print-ing Office.

————. 1990b. *Census of Population (1990). Social and Economic Characteristics. North Carolina*. Washington, D.C.: U.S. Government Printing Office.

Volkman, Toby Alice. 1990. "Visions and Revisions: Toraja Culture and the Tourist Gaze." *American Ethnologist* 17:91–120.

Wachacha, Herbert, and Yvonne Wachacha. 1981. "Tradition and Change: Tra-ditions Kept by the Snowbird Cherokees of Graham County." In *The Chero-

kee Perspective, edited by L. French and J. Hornbuckle French, 58–62. Boone, N.C.: Appalachian Consortium Press.

Walker, Willard. 1969. "Notes on Native Writing Systems and the Design of Native Literacy Programs." *Anthropological Linguistics* 11:148–66.

———. 1975. "Cherokee." In *Studies in Southeastern Indian Languages,* edited by James M. Crawford, 189–236. Athens: University of Georgia Press.

———. 1984. "Literacy, Wampums, the *gudebuk,* and How Indians in the Far Northeast Read." *Anthropological Linguistics* 26:42–52.

Walker, Willard, and James Sarbaugh. 1993. "The Early History of the Cherokee Syllabary." *Ethnohistory* 40:70–94.

White, John K. 1962. "On the Revival of Printing in the Cherokee Language." *Current Anthropology* 3:511–14.

Wogan, Peter. 1994. "Perceptions of European Literacy in Early Contact Situations." *Ethnohistory* 41:407–29.

Woodward, Grace Steele. 1963. *The Cherokees.* Norman: University of Oklahoma Press.

Woolard, Kathryn A. 1985. "Language Variation and Cultural Hegemony." *American Ethnologist* 12:738–48.

Index